AF413600

THE ILLUSION OF LUXURY

Living Beyond
Labels and Logos

TANMEENN SINGH MAKEN

Year of Publication 2025

INDIA · SINGAPORE · MALAYSIA

Declaration

This book, *The Illusion of Luxury: Living Beyond Labels and Logos*, is not intended to defame, criticize, or harm the reputation of any brands, products, or individuals. Instead, it serves as a guide to help readers adopt a balanced approach to consumption, encouraging contentment, individuality, and mindful living rather than blindly following societal trends.

All characters, scenarios, and anecdotes presented in this book are purely fictional and created for illustrative purposes. Any resemblance to real persons, living or deceased, or actual events is purely coincidental.

The book recognizes the significant contributions of brands to society, including their innovation, quality, and craftsmanship. Its aim is not to undermine their value but to empower readers to make conscious, informed choices that align with their personal values and priorities.

This work is meant to foster awareness and reflection, and it does not intend to offend, misrepresent, or cause harm to any individual, organization, or entity. The insights shared are intended to encourage readers to navigate consumer culture responsibly and thoughtfully.

I, Tanmeenn Singh Maken, declare that The Illusion of Luxury is a work born of my own research, reflections, and creative process. While inspired by real-world themes and contradictions, all characters, scenarios, and events in this book are fictional. Any resemblance to actual persons, living or deceased, is purely coincidental.

Dedication

To the ones who walk confidently without the weight of logos.

To those who find value in authenticity over appearances.

To the people who don't need brands to be seen, heard, or recognized—this book is for you.

May your self-assurance inspire others to look beyond labels and discover the beauty of true individuality.

Table of Contents

Preface 11

Acknowledgements 13

Introduction: The Allure of the Brand 15

PART I
THE ORIGINS AND PSYCHOLOGY OF BRANDED GOODS

Chapter 1   The Branding Illusion – Why We Want What We Don't Need 21

Chapter 2   The Social Dynamics of Luxury: A Need to Show Economic Power? 26

Chapter 3   The Emotional High – Temporary Happiness vs. Long-Term Contentment 31

PART II
HISTORY AND HUMAN NATURE – THE DESIRE FOR SUPERIORITY

Chapter 4   The Middle-Class Dilemma – Aspirations vs. Reality 41

Chapter 5   The Role of Influencers and Media in Shaping Aspirations 47

Chapter 6   Do the Rich Really Want to Show Off? 54

PART III
ECONOMIC AND MARKET DYNAMICS OF LUXURY

Chapter 7   Are Branded Goods a Necessity or Just a Desire? 62

Chapter 8   Lessons from Kings, Queens, and Aristocracy:
               Historical Insights on Wealth Display 68

PART IV
THE ETHICAL AND PSYCHOLOGICAL TRAP OF LUXURY GOODS

Chapter 9   Walking Billboards – The Indian Love Affair
               with Brands...76

Chapter 10   The Economics of Luxury – How Markets
               Shape Our Desires 80

Chapter 11   The Pros of Branded Goods – When Luxury
               Makes Sense...88

Chapter 12   How Brands Exploit Human Hunger for
               Superiority 94

Chapter 13   The Role of Culture and Tradition in Luxury
               Perception... 101

Chapter 14   The Role of Cultural Identity in Branded
               Goods – A Reflection of Values................................. 107

Chapter 15   Everyday Luxuries – The Subtle Art of
               Showing Off 114

Chapter 16   Luxury and Mental Health – The Hidden
               Costs of Comparison Culture.................................... 144

PART V
THE PROS AND CONS OF LUXURY GOODS

Chapter 17   The Middle-Class Illusion – Trapped in the
               Branded Goods Cycle 152

Chapter 18   The New Upscale Market Platforms – How the
               Digital Age Fuels Aspirational Buying 158

PART VI
BREAKING FREE AND FINDING REAL VALUE

Chapter 19 The Pros and Cons of Branded Goods for the Middle Class 170

Chapter 20 How Brands Exploit Human Nature – The Hidden Psychology Behind Consumerism 176

Chapter 21 The Paradox of Choice – Does More Really Make Us Happier? 183

Chapter 22 The Role of Advertising in Shaping Consumer Culture 189

Chapter 23 The Rise of Sustainable and Ethical Brands – A New Kind of Luxury 196

Chapter 24 Real Stories of Breaking Free – Case Studies of Conscious Consumers 203

Chapter 25 The Future of Luxury: Emerging Trends and Predictions 209

Chapter 26 Minimalism vs. Consumerism – A New Trend for the Middle Class? 215

Chapter 27 A Practical Guide to Conscious Consumption 223

Conclusion: Striking a Balance – Navigating the World of Branded Goods 231

Discussion Questions and Reflection Prompts 235

References and Sources 239

Preface

The inspiration for this book stems from something I have observed over the years — a growing obsession with luxury and branded goods, particularly among the middle class. In my travels and interactions with people from different walks of life, one thing has become increasingly clear: owning luxury products is no longer just a marker of wealth, but a symbol of aspiration, success, and even identity.

As someone who comes from a business industry and has built a career around understanding markets and consumer behavior, I've always been curious about the psychology behind our desires. Why do we chase after the latest designer handbag or the most expensive car? Why do we, as a society, feel the need to define ourselves by the brands we wear, drive, or own? And most importantly, what impact does this constant pursuit of luxury have on our financial well-being, emotional health, and overall happiness?

This book is not meant to be a critique of luxury itself. There is undeniable value in high-quality products and in rewarding oneself for hard work. However, it is a critical reflection on how branded goods can sometimes trap us in a cycle of endless consumption, where the more we have, the less satisfied we feel. Through this work, I aim to explore the fine line between **wanting** something and **needing** it — between finding joy in luxury and being consumed by it.

I was motivated to write this book because I saw the middle class, particularly in India, gets caught in this cycle. Many of us work tirelessly, save diligently, and then spend lavishly on things that promise happiness but deliver only fleeting satisfaction. This is not just an economic issue; it is a cultural and psychological phenomenon that affects how we view success, how we interact with others, and even how we define our self-worth.

In these pages, I hope to offer an understanding of why we are drawn to luxury, how marketing and societal pressures fuel our desires, and how we can regain control over our consumption. Through personal stories, research, and reflections, I want to encourage you, the reader, to rethink your relationship with branded goods — not to reject them entirely, but to engage with them more mindfully.

Ultimately, this book is an invitation to break free from the illusion of luxury and to explore a life where fulfilment comes not from the brands we own, but from the values we hold and the experiences we create.

Tanmeenn Singh Maken

2025

Acknowledgements

Writing this book has been an incredible journey, and I would like to extend my deepest gratitude to those who helped me along the way.

To my family, whose love and support have been my anchor throughout this process — thank you for your patience, encouragement, and understanding. To my parents, for instilling in me the values of hard work and integrity, and to my wife and children, for being my greatest source of inspiration.

To my friends and colleagues, thank you for your insights, feedback, and conversations that shaped many of the ideas within these pages. Your perspectives have been invaluable.

I am also grateful to Aadishri Yadav (editor), and everyone involved in the production of this book. Your hard work and attention to detail have brought this vision to life.

Lastly, to the readers of this book — it is my hope that these pages will resonate with you and spark new thoughts about the true meaning of luxury, success, and happiness.

Tanmeenn Singh Maken

2025

Introduction: The Allure of the Brand

The shiny logo on a handbag, the distinctive tick on a pair of shoes, the elegant curves of a luxury car — they all speak a universal language. For some, these symbols represent success, wealth, and social standing. For others, they embody aspirations, dreams, and sometimes, a distant reality. In India, where social status often feels intertwined with material possessions, branded goods have become more than just items—they're a declaration of identity. But the question remains: Why do we desire them so much?

The attraction towards luxury brands grows in tandem with the expanding dreams and rising incomes of the rapidly growing Indian middle class. From designer saris to high-end smartphones, branded goods have become a symbol of having "arrived." They signal to the world that you've made it. But behind this glamour lies a hidden trap — a psychological, social, and financial trap that many fall into without realizing its consequences.

Take Rakesh, for example. A marketing manager living in the bustling streets of Delhi, Rakesh had always been practical with money. He grew up in a middle-class household where every rupee was spent carefully, and savings were prioritized. Now, as a father of two and the sole breadwinner of his family, he was still cautious. His biggest focus was his children's education and securing a better future for them.

But over time, Rakesh noticed a shift in the world around him. On his social media feeds, he saw his colleagues and old school friends flaunting their new branded watches, the latest iPhones, or their vacations to Dubai and Europe. At family weddings, his relatives discussed their new purchases — from luxury handbags to imported cars. Slowly,

Rakesh started to feel inadequate. He worked hard, yet he felt like he wasn't achieving enough. Was he missing out? Did his lack of branded goods make him seem less successful?

It started small — a branded pair of shoes he couldn't really afford but justified as a "reward" for his hard work. When his colleagues noticed the shoes complimenting him on his "great taste," he felt a rush of pride. The recognition was immediate, but fleeting. Next came a branded watch, then a designer handbag for his wife, and soon Rakesh started scouring online platforms for the latest luxury goods, now caught in a cycle of buying to maintain appearances. What began as a desire for recognition soon turned into a financial burden.

As the EMI payments piled up, Rakesh started feeling the pinch. His monthly expenses were rising, but his satisfaction with these branded goods seemed to evaporate quickly. Each new purchase brought a brief moment of happiness, but the void only grew deeper. Rakesh, like many in the Indian middle class, had been lured into the belief that branded goods were a marker of success. But in reality, these items were eating away at his financial peace and mental well-being.

Rakesh's story is not unique. Many middle-class families across urban and semi-urban India are also caught in a similar predicament. The pressure to keep up with social expectations, to show that they've "arrived," often leads to unnecessary spending on branded goods. But are these goods truly a reflection of success? Or is this simply an illusion created by society, by marketing, by a relentless need to fit in?

This book aims to explore the deeper questions behind the allure of branded goods. It's not just about understanding consumerism but about digging into the psychology, culture, and economics that make these items so desirable. Why do the wealthy flaunt their branded possessions? How has the middle class become trapped in this race for status symbols? And, most importantly, how do brands exploit these desires to fuel their profits?

From the grand palaces of ancient Indian kings and queens, where opulence was a sign of power, to the modern-day luxury brands that adorn the wealthy, the desire to be seen as superior has always existed. While the rich can indulge in these luxuries without a second thought, the middle class often finds itself financially stretched, trying to maintain an image that may not even bring genuine happiness or fulfilment.

As we journey through this book, we'll uncover the true cost of luxury. Not just in rupees, but in time, mental peace, and emotional well-being. We'll explore the roots of this obsession with brands, how it evolved over time, and why it's now part of the Indian middle-class identity. Most importantly, we'll challenge the notion that branded goods are necessary for success and examine whether there's a way to break free from this cycle of desire.

Finally, this book is meant to empower you — the reader. By the end, you will have a clearer understanding of why luxury, as it's sold to us, is often an illusion. You'll discover ways to redefine success and contentment, to shift your focus from materialism to what truly matters — experiences, personal growth, and peace of mind.

Let's embark on this journey together, as we uncover the layers of shiny logos and expensive brands, and realize that happiness and success do not come from what we own, but from how we live.

PART I

THE ORIGINS AND PSYCHOLOGY OF BRANDED GOODS

Chapter 1

The Branding Illusion – Why We Want What We Don't Need

In the busy markets of Connaught Place or the flashing malls of Bengaluru, one thing becomes immediately apparent — the logos. Whether it's the gold emblem of Gucci, the iconic "LV" of Louis Vuitton, or the swoosh of Nike, brands have an unmistakable presence.

But here's the question we need to ask ourselves: why do these logos hold so much power over us?

For many Indian consumers, the answer seems obvious: branded goods mean quality. But deep down, there's more to it than that. These logos are more than just guarantees of good craftsmanship or durability. They are symbols of status, wealth, and aspiration. When we buy a branded product, we aren't just paying for the item — we are paying for what it says about us.

The Day Riya Bought Her First Branded Handbag

Let's start with a story that might sound familiar to many of us. Riya, a 28-year-old marketing executive in Mumbai, had been eyeing a branded handbag for months. It was a stunning, leather crossbody bag from a luxury European brand, and it had caught her attention every time she walked through the mall.

At first, she dismissed the idea of buying it. The price tag was outrageous — ₹35,000 for a handbag! That's more than her rent. But every time she scrolled through Instagram, there it was — influencers and celebrities showing off their new "it" bags. Riya couldn't help but feel that maybe, just maybe, she deserved to own something like that. After all, she had been working hard, saving up, and wasn't she entitled to reward herself?

One day, after receiving a year-end bonus at work, she finally gave in. Walking out of the store with the gleaming shopping bag in hand, she felt a rush of excitement. She had arrived, or so she thought. The moment she walked into her office with that bag, she noticed her colleagues taking a second glance. Someone even commented, "Wow, nice bag! Is that the latest collection?" That moment of recognition made Riya feel validated, like she was part of an exclusive club.

But as the weeks went by, something strange happened. The excitement of owning the bag began to fade. Slowly, it just became... another bag.

The compliments stopped, the initial thrill was gone, and Riya was left with was a dent in her bank account. She realized that while the bag had brought her a momentary sense of achievement; it had added no real value to her life. In fact, she was now stressing about her next credit card bill. Was it really worth it?

The Social Pressure to Own Branded Goods

Riya's story is not unique. Across India, in cities large and small, people like her are often caught up in the allure of branded goods. Whether it's the latest iPhone, a pair of Ray-Ban sunglasses, or an expensive watch, the desire to own something branded is almost universal. But why?

Part of the reason lies in the **social expectation** of appearing successful. For many Indians, branded goods aren't just about personal satisfaction — they're about signaling wealth and status to others. It's why we see people flaunting their new purchases on social media, tagging themselves in luxury stores, and showing off the latest gadgets at weddings or parties. There's an unspoken competition going on, and branded goods are the scoreboard.

For the middle class in India, this pressure is especially intense. Unlike the rich, who can afford to buy these items effortlessly, the middle class often stretches beyond their means to keep up with the trend. We've all heard stories of people buying the latest iPhone on EMI or taking loans to purchase luxury cars. But at what cost? Is the temporary satisfaction worth the financial strain?

The Branding Illusion: What We Really Buy Into

When we buy a branded product, we're not just buying an item — we're buying into a story. Brands have mastered the art of storytelling, convincing us that their products represent more than just material goods. Take, for example, an advertisement for a luxury car. The ad doesn't just show the features of the car; it shows a successful, well-dressed man driving down an empty road, looking out over a beautiful landscape. It's not about the car — it's about the lifestyle. It tells us that if we buy this car, we too will be successful, respected, and admired.

Brands, particularly luxury brands, play on our deepest desires — the desire to be seen, respected, and admired. In a country like India, where social status plays a significant role in shaping our identity, this appeal is even more powerful. Owning branded goods makes us feel like we've made it, like we've crossed a social barrier. But here's the uncomfortable truth: often, it's just an illusion.

Think about it: how long does the satisfaction of a branded product last? A few weeks? A couple of months? Then what? Most of us quickly move on to wanting the next big thing, chasing the next "hit" of satisfaction. It's a never-ending cycle, that drains our finances and leaves us constantly feeling like we need more.

Do We Really Need It, or Are We Just Trapped?

As Indian consumers, we need to ask ourselves: do we really need these branded goods, or are we just trapped in a cycle of wanting them? Most branded products aren't about utility — they're about identity. And while it's okay to indulge in something nice every now and then, we must be cautious of tying our self-worth to what we own.

For people like Riya, the realization came too late. The handbag that once seemed like a symbol of success now felt like a financial burden. But the bigger burden was the mindset — the belief that she needed branded goods to feel good about herself. Breaking free from that belief is the first step toward true financial freedom and emotional peace.

The Real Cost of Branded Goods

In a country where the majority is still struggling to make ends meet, it's worth reflecting on how much we, as middle-class consumers, are willing to sacrifice for the sake of owning something branded.

Think about the stress that comes with paying off an EMI for a product that, deep down, you know you didn't need. Think about the fleeting happiness you get from showing off a new purchase, only to be replaced by the pressure to keep up with the next trend. This is the actual cost of branded goods — a cost that most middle-class Indians cannot afford.

Conclusion: Breaking Free from the Illusion

So why do we want what we don't need? The answer lies in a combination of social pressure, clever marketing, and our own insecurities. But the good news is that we can break free from this cycle. By shifting our mindset and focusing on what truly brings value to our lives — experiences, relationships, and personal growth — we can find happiness without the need for logos or luxury.

The next time you're tempted to buy something branded, ask yourself: am I buying this for myself, or for the approval of others? The answer might surprise you.

Chapter 2

The Social Dynamics of Luxury: A Need to Show Economic Power?

Ravi, a 32-year-old software engineer from Bengaluru, wasn't someone who cared much about brands. Coming from a humble background, Ravi valued saving money more than showing off wealth. However, after switching jobs and joining a well-known multinational company, Ravi's world begun to change. His new colleagues all seemed to live in a different universe — one filled with high-end watches, the latest smartphones, and expensive cars. They weren't just talking about work in the cafeteria; they were also talking about their newest purchases.

Soon, Ravi began to feel the pressure. During one lunch break, a colleague asked him why he was still using an old phone model, when everyone else had upgraded to the latest iPhone. Ravi laughed it off, but the question made him feel insecure. The idea that he needed to fit in — to be part of this new social circle — began to consume his thoughts. A week later, Ravi found himself buying the new iPhone on an EMI plan. Even though it stretched his budget, he told himself it was necessary to keep up appearances at work.

This story resonates with many middle-class Indians. As society becomes increasingly obsessed with material success, the pressure to fit in with those around us can be overwhelming. Whether it's in the office, at a family wedding, or even scrolling through social media, the message is simple: If you don't have the latest gadgets, clothes, or accessories, you risk being left out.

The Power of Social Proof: Why We Feel the Pressure

One of the most powerful forces driving the need for branded goods is **social proof** — the psychological phenomenon where people imitate the behaviors of those around them to fit in. In India, this concept is magnified by the strong importance placed on community and social status. Whether in our neighborhoods, workplaces, or extended families, there's an unspoken expectation to keep up with those around us.

For instance, think about the pressure that builds around weddings in India. People expect guests to dress in their finest, and relatives often engage in quiet competition about who wears the most expensive saree, who arrives in the newest car, or who gifts the most lavish presents. The middle class, in particular, gets caught in this cycle — striving to keep up with the social expectations set by those around them, often stretching their finances to do so.

Ravi's decision to buy a new phone wasn't about the phone itself. It was about the need to fit in. The same logic applies to countless other purchases we make. Whether it's buying a new watch, upgrading to a bigger car, or wearing a designer dress to a function, the underlying motivation is often the same: we don't want to be seen as "less than" the people around us.

Social Media: Amplifying the Pressure

In India, the rise of social media has only magnified this pressure. Platforms like Instagram, Facebook, and even WhatsApp have become windows to other's lifestyle. The curated, filtered lives we see online often portray a world where everyone seems to have it all — the best vacations, the finest clothes, the latest gadgets.

The more we scroll, the more we're convinced that we're falling behind. Social media has created a constant comparison loop, where we measure our success against the posts and stories of others. But what we often forget that social media only shows us one side of the story — the glamorous, polished side. We don't see the credit card bills, the financial strain, or the anxiety that might be hiding behind that perfect Instagram shot.

Consider Meera, a 29-year-old marketing executive in Mumbai. Meera had always been content with her modest lifestyle until she started following influencers on Instagram. Every day, she saw pictures of people wearing the latest fashion, dining at fancy restaurants, and traveling to exotic destinations. Soon, Meera felt her own life paled in comparison. Even though she couldn't afford it, she began purchasing designer clothes and dining out at high-end restaurants just to keep up with the image of success she saw online. Social media created a new standard to which she felt compelled to follow — and it was a standard she couldn't sustain.

The "Keeping Up with the Joneses" Effect

In urban India, there's a common phrase used to describe this phenomenon: **keeping up with the Joneses.** This term refers to the social pressure to match the lifestyle of those around you. Whether it's your neighbors, colleagues, or relatives, the desire to keep up with what others have can drive people to make financial decisions that aren't always in their best interest.

Take the example of Rajesh, a small business owner in Delhi. He lived in a middle-class neighborhood where most families had similar income levels. But when his next-door neighbor bought a new car, Rajesh felt the pressure to upgrade his own vehicle, even though his current one was still in great condition. A few months later, Rajesh took out a loan to buy a new car. In doing so, he stretched his finances, but he felt relieved that he had "kept up" with his neighbour. This cycle of one-upmanship is a reality many middle-class families face. The constant comparison drives people to spend beyond their means, leading to stress, debt, and financial insecurity.

The Emotional Toll of Fitting In

While owning branded goods or upgrading to the latest gadgets might provide a momentary sense of belonging, the emotional toll of keeping up with others is often far greater than we realize. The constant pressure to fit in, to match the success of others, can lead to anxiety, dissatisfaction, and even burnout.

For many middle-class Indians, the stress of keeping up with social expectations is an everyday reality. The need to maintain a certain image — whether it's at work, in social circles, or within extended families — often comes at the expense of mental peace. People find themselves working longer hours, taking on more financial burden, and sacrificing their emotional well-being just to keep up appearances.

Is It Worth It?

We need to ask ourselves a simple question: Is it worth it? Is the temporary satisfaction of owning a branded product or upgrading our lifestyle really worth the long-term stress and financial strain?

For Ravi, the realization came too late. After months of making EMI payments on his new phone, he started to regret his decision. The excitement of owning the latest gadget faded, leaving Ravi with the burden of debt. He realized that the pressure to fit in had clouded his judgment — and it was a mistake he didn't want to repeat.

Conclusion: Finding Peace in Your Own Path

The truth is, the pressure to fit in is not going away anytime soon. In a society where social status is often tied to material possessions, the desire to keep up with others will always exist. But this doesn't mean that we need to comply. By recognizing the forces at play — social proof, comparison, and social media — we can take a step back and make more conscious decisions about what we truly need and value in life.

we can choose to find peace in our own path, instead of letting others' opinion affects our decision making in buying goods and services. We don't need to follow the crowd or buy into the branding illusion to feel successful. True contentment comes from living authentically and making decisions that align with our values — not the values of others.

Chapter 3

The Emotional High – Temporary Happiness vs. Long-Term Contentment

If you've ever bought something expensive — maybe the latest phone, a designer dress, or a luxury watch — you're probably familiar with the rush of excitement that comes with it. The moment you unwrap that item, there's a sense of pride, a boost in mood, and maybe even a bit of confidence that wasn't there before. You look forward to showing it off to friends, colleagues, or family. At that moment, it feels like life has improved. But after a few days, that excitement fades, doesn't it?

This is the emotional cycle that many of us go through when we purchase branded or luxury goods. At first, there's a surge of happiness, but soon after, the novelty wears off, and what remains is often a feeling of dissatisfaction — or worse, the urge to buy something else to get that high again.

In this chapter, we'll explore the psychology behind why luxury goods bring only temporary happiness and how true contentment often comes from things that cannot be bought.

The First Rush: Excitement and Status Boost

Let's take the example of Sunil, a 35-year-old IT professional in Pune. Sunil had been saving up for months to buy a luxury watch. He saw it as a symbol of his hard work and success. When he finally made the purchase, the thrill was undeniable. The day he wore it to work, he noticed his colleagues' approving glances. One even asked, "Is that the new model? Must've cost a fortune!" Sunil felt proud, his self-esteem boosted by the recognition.

This is what psychologists call the **"reward response"** — the brain's release of dopamine, a neurotransmitter associated with pleasure and satisfaction. The act of purchasing, especially something expensive and coveted, triggers this response. It's the brain's way of rewarding us for achieving something we desire. And in Sunil's case, the acknowledgment of others further fueled this sense of accomplishment.

However, this emotional high doesn't last long.

The Law of Diminishing Returns: The Fade of Satisfaction

A few weeks after buying his watch, Sunil's excitement started to wane. The watch, which once felt like the ultimate symbol of his success, had now become just another accessory. His colleagues had moved on, and so had he. The initial rush of pride and validation he had felt was gone. The watch was still there, but the feeling it once gave him had disappeared.

This is a classic case of **Hedonic Adaptation**, also known as the **Hedonic Treadmill**. It indicates that humans tend to return to a baseline level of happiness quickly after experiencing positive or negative events. In simpler terms, no matter how exciting or luxurious the purchase, we eventually get used to it, and it no longer brings us the joy it initially did.

For many of us, the momentary thrill of buying something new quickly fades, and we find ourselves longing for the next new thing. It's why, after buying a new phone or car, we soon find ourselves browsing for the next model. The satisfaction is always temporary, and we're always looking for the next item to fill that emotional void.

What We Really Seek: Validation, Status, and Belonging

If we peel back the layers of why we chase branded goods, we often find that it's not the item itself that we desire. It's what the item represents. In Indian society, which is deeply influenced by social hierarchies, possessions can become markers of success and status. When we buy luxury items, we're often seeking validation, recognition, or a sense of belonging in a certain social group.

Take the case of Priya, a 28-year-old media executive in Delhi. Priya wasn't into fashion or luxury goods — that is until she started attending high-profile industry events. Surrounded by colleagues and influencers dressed in designer clothes, carrying expensive handbags, Priya felt out of place. So, she began buying luxury items, not because she wanted them, but because she wanted to fit in. She felt that owning those items would give her a sense of belonging and respect in her social circle.

Priya's story of falling into a trap of expensive buying is not new. The validation from others becomes more important than the utility of the product itself.

Chasing Happiness: Why Material Goods Can't Fill the Void

There's a common belief that buying things will make us happier. Advertisements reinforce this idea — that owning a luxury car, the latest phone, or a branded outfit will somehow elevate our lives. But research shows that material possessions only bring fleeting happiness. Once the novelty wears off, we're left with the same emotional baseline we had before the purchase.

True, lasting contentment comes not from what we own, but from the experiences we have, the relationships we build, and the sense of purpose we cultivate. A study conducted by researchers at Cornell University found that **experiences bring people more happiness than possessions.** The reason? Experiences foster personal growth, create memories, and build social connections — all of which contribute to lasting fulfilment.

The Emotional Debt: What We Sacrifice for Branded Goods

There's another side to the story that's often overlooked: the emotional debt that comes with trying to keep up with branded goods. For many middle-class Indians, buying luxury items means taking out loans, using credit cards, or cutting back on essential savings. While the initial purchase might bring happiness, the stress of paying off those items can lead to anxiety and regret.

Rajesh, a 40-year-old businessman from Hyderabad, learned this lesson the hard way. After buying a luxury car on EMI to "keep up" with his wealthy business associates, he found himself constantly stressed about the monthly payments. What was once a symbol of success soon became a financial burden. He realized that the car, which had once brought him joy, was now a source of constant worry.

This is the reality for many middle-class consumers who stretch their finances to buy luxury goods. The emotional toll of debt and financial strain often outweighs the temporary satisfaction of owning the product.

The Shift: Finding Long-Term Contentment

If luxury goods bring only temporary happiness, then where can we find lasting contentment? The answer lies not in what we buy, but in how we live. Instead of chasing material possessions, we can focus on what truly matters: experiences, personal growth, and relationships.

For Ritu, a 33-year-old teacher from Chandigarh, the shift happened when she stopped chasing brands and started focusing on experiences. Instead of buying a new car or upgrading her wardrobe, she invested in a solo trip to the mountains. That experience, she says, brought her more joy than any material possession ever could. The memories she made, the sense of accomplishment she felt, and the personal growth she experienced were far more valuable than anything she could have bought.

Conclusion: Moving Beyond Temporary Highs

It's natural to want nice things. There's nothing wrong with enjoying the finer things in life. But when we tie our happiness and self-worth to material possessions, we set ourselves up for disappointment. Branded goods may bring temporary excitement, but true contentment comes from within — from living authentically, building meaningful relationships, and focusing on personal growth.

The next time you find yourself tempted by a shiny new product, take a moment to ask yourself: Is this purchase going to bring me long-term joy, or am I chasing a fleeting high? The answer might surprise you.

End of Part I: The Origins and Psychology of Branded Goods

In Part I, we examined the psychological and social drivers behind the desire for branded goods. Luxury is often marketed not just as a product but as an identity, leading people to believe that branded items can provide them with status, happiness, or even purpose. The takeaways include:

1. **The Branding Illusion**: Brands construct an image of exclusivity and necessity, convincing people that ownership equates to worth. This creates an illusion that branded goods are essential for self-identity.

2. **Social Validation**: In many societies, luxury items have become symbols of social status and economic power. They are often used to convey success, leading people to believe that these items are indicators of personal achievement.

3. **The Fleeting Emotional High**: Although buying luxury items can bring temporary excitement, this feeling quickly fades. This cycle often leaves people wanting more as the initial satisfaction diminishes.

PART II

HISTORY AND HUMAN NATURE –
THE DESIRE FOR SUPERIORITY

Chapter 4

The Middle-Class
Dilemma – Aspirations vs. Reality

Sanjay grew up in a small town, but like many in India's rapidly growing middle class, he had big dreams. After completing his engineering degree, he moved to Bengaluru, where he quickly found a job at a tech startup. Over the next few years, Sanjay's career blossomed, and he was soon earning more than he had ever imagined. But with this newfound success came a different kind of pressure — the pressure to "look the part."

Every day on his commute to work, Sanjay noticed the cars his colleagues drove: sleek sedans and luxury SUVs. He saw the watches they wore, the expensive clothes, and the designer bags they carried. Slowly but surely, he began to feel inadequate. He had worked hard to reach this point, but why didn't it feel like enough? Why did he feel like he was falling behind?

In his mind, Sanjay's success didn't fully count unless it looked like success. And so, like many others in the middle class, he began spending on things he once considered extravagant. A new car, a fancy phone, designer clothes — the shopping never seemed to end. But even after these purchases, the feeling of inadequacy remained. Instead of feeling proud of his achievements, Sanjay found himself stressed about the bills piling up and the constant desire for more.

The Aspirational Trap: When Success is Never Enough

Sanjay's story resonates with many, particularly those in the Indian middle class. As incomes rise and job opportunities expand, many middle-class families find themselves caught between aspirations and reality. On one hand, they're proud of the progress they've made, working hard to achieve their dreams, often rising from humble beginnings. On the other hand, they feel a constant pressure to keep up with their peers, to prove that they've "made it."

But here's the problem: aspirations are a moving target. The more we achieve, the more we want. And in today's consumer-driven society, success is often measured not by how hard we've worked or how far we've come, but by what we own. For the middle class, this creates an endless cycle of wanting more — more branded goods, more luxurious experiences, more ways to signal success to the world.

But is this really what success looks like?

Keeping Up with the Upper Class: The Social Divide

In India, the gap between the middle class and the wealthy is significant. While the middle class has seen tremendous growth over the past few decades, the wealthiest individuals and families continue to pull ahead, setting the tone for what "success" looks like. Bollywood movies, ads, and social media all portray the lifestyles of the rich and famous, creating an unrealistic standard against which everyone compares their own progress.

This creates what sociologists call a **"status divide"**. Middle-class individuals, like Sanjay, often feel pressure to emulate the lifestyles of the wealthy, even if it means stretching their finances. The problem is, while the wealthy can afford to buy luxury goods without worrying about the price, the middle class often finds itself taking on debt or sacrificing savings to keep up.

Take the case of Priya, a teacher in Pune. Priya loved her job, but after seeing her colleagues arrive at work with luxury handbags and expensive shoes, she started feeling out of place. Even though she was financially stable, she felt a growing desire to buy into the lifestyle of those around her. So, Priya began shopping for designer clothes, even if it meant putting her purchases on a credit card. At first, it felt empowering. But soon, the credit card bills started piling up, and Priya realized she was living beyond her means — all for the sake of appearances.

The Cost of Keeping Up: Financial Strain and Emotional Burnout

For many middle-class families, the cost of keeping up with social expectations goes far beyond the price tag of luxury goods. The emotional and financial toll of constantly trying to match the lifestyle of others can be overwhelming.

For instance, Sanjay's initial excitement after buying his new car quickly faded when he realized how much he was paying for monthly EMI payments. What was once a symbol of success soon became a source of stress. And Sanjay isn't alone. Across urban India, middle-class families are increasingly relying on **EMIs, loans, and credit cards** to purchase luxury items they can't really afford.

But what's the actual cost of this lifestyle? Research shows that **financial stress** is one of the leading causes of anxiety, depression, and relationship problems. The pressure to maintain a certain image can lead to **emotional burnout**, leaving individuals feeling trapped in a cycle of work, spend, repeat. Instead of enjoying the fruits of their labor, many middle-class families are left feeling dissatisfied, constantly chasing the next purchase to fill the emotional void.

The Reality Check: Do We Really Need It?

It's easy to get caught up in the excitement of new purchases, especially when branded goods are marketed as symbols of success. But here's the question we need to ask ourselves: **Do we really need it?** Or are we simply buying into the idea that success equals more stuff?

For people like Sanjay and Priya, the realization often comes too late. After months of making payments on their luxury purchases, they start to realize that the excitement has faded, but the bills remain. They realize that the joy they expected from owning these items was temporary — and that real contentment can't be bought.

Breaking Free from the Aspiration Trap

If you've ever found yourself feeling pressured to buy something just because others around you have it, you're not alone. The question now arises, how do we break from this cycle of aspirational buying? Here are a few steps to help you do just that:

1. **Shift Your Focus:** Instead of focusing on what you don't have, focus on what you've already achieved. Remind yourself of how far you've come and the work you've put in to get there. Success is about progress, not possessions.

2. **Practice Gratitude:** One of the simplest ways to combat the aspiration trap is to practice gratitude. Take time each day to appreciate what you have — whether it's your health, your family, or your job. The more you focus on what you're grateful for, the less you'll feel the need to chase after material things.

3. **Create a Budget That Reflects Your Values:** It's okay to spend money on things that matter to you, but make sure your spending aligns with your values. Instead of buying things to impress others, spend money on things that bring you genuine joy — whether that's travel, education, or experiences with loved ones.

4. **Learn to Say No:** It can be hard to resist the pressure to keep up with others, but learning to say no is a powerful tool. Whether it's turning down an invitation to a lavish event or resisting the urge to buy something you don't need, saying no helps you take control of your own financial decisions.

5. **Focus on Experiences, Not Things:** Studies have shown that experiences bring more long-lasting happiness than material goods. Instead of buying the latest gadget or luxury item, invest in experiences that enrich your life — whether that's a weekend getaway, a new hobby, or quality time with family and friends.

Conclusion: Finding Peace in Simplicity

Success isn't about how much you own. It's about how you feel. And for many the constant chase for more leaves them feeling empty and exhausted. By shifting the focus away from material possessions and towards what truly matters — personal growth, relationships, and inner peace — it's possible to break free from the aspirational trap and find true contentment.

For Sanjay, this realization came after months of financial stress. He eventually sold his luxury car, paid off his debts, and started focusing on his savings and long-term goals. Today, he feels more secure and content, not because of what he owns, but because of the peace that comes with living within his means.

Chapter 5

The Role of Influencers and Media in Shaping Aspirations

Ankita, a 25-year-old content writer in Mumbai, loved spending time on Instagram. What began as a way to unwind after work quickly turned into hours of scrolling through perfectly curated feeds.

Influencers she followed were constantly posting pictures of luxurious vacations, designer clothes, and branded gadgets. Ankita couldn't help but compare her own life to theirs — her local cafe lunch didn't seem as glamorous as the influencers' fancy brunches in five-star hotels, and her wardrobe felt inadequate compared to their designer outfits.

Before long, Ankita found herself saving up to buy the same products she saw in their posts — the same lipstick, the same handbag, the same smartphone case. She even began using the hashtags they used, hoping to feel more connected to the glamorous lives they portrayed. Yet, despite all her purchases, she couldn't shake the feeling that she wasn't enough. How was it that these influencers, who she didn't even know personally, were shaping her entire lifestyle?

Ankita's story is increasingly common among young Indians. In a world dominated by social media, influencers and celebrities play a powerful role in shaping our aspirations, our desires, and even our sense of self-worth. In this chapter, we will explore how influencers and media influence the middle class's obsession with branded goods, and how this constant exposure can trap people in an endless cycle of comparison and consumption.

The Power of Influencers: A New Type of Role Model

Influencers are today's cultural tastemakers. With massive followings on platforms like Instagram, YouTube, and Twitter, influencers have the power to shape trends, spark new desires, and create entire markets. What sets them apart from traditional celebrities is their relatability — unlike movie stars or business moguls, influencers present themselves as ordinary people living extraordinary lives. They post pictures from their homes, share snippets of their daily routines, and often interact directly with their followers.

For Ankita, it was this sense of relatability that drew her in. She didn't just see influencers as untouchable celebrities — she saw them as people just like her, only with better clothes, more exciting lives, and access to luxury goods. And if they could achieve that lifestyle, why couldn't she?

Influencers have perfected the art of **aspirational marketing** — making their followers believe that they too can have the same glamorous lifestyle if they buy the same products. Whether it's skincare, clothing, technology, or even food, influencers know how to tap into the desires of their audience, making branded goods seem like the gateway to a better, more successful life.

The Illusion of Perfection: Behind the Filter

Many middle-class consumers don't understand that influencers carefully curate their content. The glamorous posts we see on social media are often the result of **sponsored partnerships**, where influencers are paid to promote products or services. Behind every candid photo, there's often a business arrangement where the influencer is paid to make the product appear desirable.

For example, when Ankita purchased a branded handbag after seeing it featured in multiple influencer posts, she wasn't aware that those influencers were likely paid to showcase the product. What appeared to be a genuine recommendation was, in reality, a well-coordinated marketing strategy.

The images we see on social media are heavily filtered and edited to look flawless. Influencers and celebrities carefully choose the best angles, lighting, and even touch-ups to present an idealized version of themselves and their lives. This creates a **"highlight reel"** effect — we only see the best moments, never the struggles, insecurities, or challenges that these influencers face in their real lives.

This is particularly damaging for middle-class consumers who compare their own reality to the perfect, branded lives they see online. What they don't realize is that this perfection is an illusion, and chasing after it can lead to emotional exhaustion and financial strain.

Social Media and the Need for Validation

In today's world, **social media validation** has become a powerful driving force behind consumer behavior. The number of likes, comments, and shares a post receives often serves as a measure of social approval. For many users, buying branded goods and sharing them online is a way to seek validation from their peers and followers.

Ankita experienced this firsthand when she began posting pictures of her new purchases on Instagram. She enjoyed the flood of comments praising her for her "amazing taste" or asking where she bought her new dress. The positive feedback felt like a reward, making her feel seen and appreciated. But this validation was short-lived. Soon, she found herself posting something new to keep the likes and comments coming. It became a cycle — buy, post, get validation, and repeat.

Social media platforms are designed to fuel this cycle of consumption. By constantly exposing users to posts showcasing luxury goods, high-end experiences, and branded lifestyles, platforms encourage users to seek the same validation through their own purchases. It's a form of **social currency** — the more branded goods you display, the more validation you receive from your online community.

The Comparison Trap: When Everyone Else Seems to Have More

One of the most damaging aspects of social media is the **comparison trap** — the tendency to compare our own lives to the lives of others based on what we see online. This trap is rather harmful because social media presents an unrealistic view of reality.

For middle-class Indians like Ankita, it's easy to feel like you're falling behind when every scroll reveals someone else's vacation photos, new car, or luxury purchase. Even if you're financially stable, social media can create a sense of inadequacy, making you feel like you're not doing enough or owning enough to be considered successful.

The comparison trap can also lead to **impulsive spending**. Research shows that people who frequently use social media are more likely to make impulse purchases, often driven by the desire to keep up with what they see online. For Ankita, this meant buying things she didn't necessarily need, simply because she wanted to match the lifestyle of the influencers she followed.

The Emotional Toll of Chasing Perfection

The constant exposure to luxury goods, branded lifestyles, and influencer recommendations takes a toll on mental and emotional well-being. For many middle-class individuals, the pressure to keep up with these unrealistic standards can lead to feelings of anxiety, low self-esteem, and dissatisfaction with their own lives.

Ankita realized this when, after months of chasing after branded goods and spending her hard-earned money on luxury items, she still didn't feel fulfilled. The validation she sought from social media was fleeting, and the material goods she bought only brought temporary satisfaction. She felt trapped in a cycle of comparison, constantly measuring herself against the impossible standards set by influencers and celebrities.

This emotional toll isn't unique to Ankita. Across urban India, middle-class consumers are increasingly feeling the pressure to live up to the image of perfection presented on social media. The result? A growing sense of dissatisfaction with their own lives, financial stress, and emotional burnout.

Breaking Free from the Influence

If you find yourself caught in the influencer trap — constantly comparing your life to others and feeling pressured to buy branded goods — you're not alone. The good news is that it's possible to break free from this cycle. Here are a few strategies to help:

1. **Unfollow Influencers Who Trigger Comparison:** If you notice that certain influencers make you feel inadequate or trigger the desire to spend on things you don't need, it's time to hit the unfollow button. Curate your social media feed to include accounts that inspire positivity, creativity, and personal growth.

2. **Limit Your Social Media Time:** The more time you spend scrolling through social media, the more likely you are to fall into the comparison trap. Set limits on how much time you spend online and make sure to engage in activities that bring you joy and fulfillment outside of social media.

3. **Focus on What Brings You True Happiness:** Instead of chasing after the latest trends, focus on what genuinely brings you joy and fulfillment. Whether it's spending time with family, pursuing a hobby, or traveling to new places, prioritize experiences and relationships over material possessions.

4. **Be Mindful of Sponsored Content:** Remember that many influencers receive payment to promote the products they feature. Just because something looks good on social media doesn't mean you need to buy it. Always ask yourself if a purchase aligns with your values and needs before making a decision.

5. **Practice Gratitude:** Instead of focusing on what you don't have, take time each day to appreciate what you do have. Practicing gratitude can shift your mindset away from comparison and help you find contentment in your own life.

Conclusion: Taking Control of Your Aspirations

The power of influencers and social media is undeniable, but so is your ability to take control of your own aspirations. By recognizing the influence of social media and making conscious decisions about what truly matters to you, it's possible to break free from the comparison trap and find contentment in your own journey.

Ankita eventually realized that chasing branded goods wouldn't bring her the happiness she sought. She took a step back from social media, began focusing on her career goals, and started valuing experiences over material possessions. In doing so, she found a sense of peace and fulfillment that no amount of branded goods could provide.

Chapter 6

Do the Rich Really Want to Show Off?

Rohit was a successful businessman from Gurgaon. He had worked his way up from a modest background to build a thriving export business. Over the years, his wealth grew, and so did his collection of branded goods. His house was filled with luxury furniture, his driveway had not one but two high-end cars, and his closet was stocked with designer clothes and accessories. Whenever he attended social events, people would often compliment him on his expensive watch or ask about his latest luxury vacation.

But despite all the admiration and attention he received, Rohit sometimes wondered: Was he buying these things because he truly wanted them, or because he wanted others to see him as successful?

This is a question that many wealthy individuals, whether consciously or unconsciously, grapple with. For the rich, branded goods often go beyond simple purchases — they are symbols of achievement, status, and social power. But the question remains: Do the rich buy these goods to flaunt their wealth, or is there something deeper at play?

The Need for Recognition: Status Symbols in Indian Society

In India, where social status is tied to material wealth, luxury goods have long been a way for the wealthy to distinguish themselves from others. From ancient times, kings and queens adorned themselves with jewels and gold, not just for personal enjoyment, but also for projecting power and superiority. This tradition has carried forward into modern society, where wealth is signaled through expensive cars, branded clothes, and lavish homes.

For the wealthy, **status symbols** are a way of communicating their success to the world. It's not just about owning the best or most expensive things — it's about being seen owning them. Branded goods become a way to command admiration from others in a culture where recognition and respect are closely linked to one's social standing,

Take the case of Sushma, a well-known socialite in Delhi. For her, attending a function without wearing designer clothes or the latest jewelry would be unthinkable. The expectation, both from her peers and from herself, is that she must always look the part of a successful and wealthy woman. And so, every year, she spends a fortune on designer sarees, handbags, and accessories, not because she necessarily wants them, but because she feels the need to maintain her image.

This need for recognition drives much of the luxury consumption among the rich. But the question we must ask is: **Does owning these items truly bring satisfaction, or are they just a way to fill an emotional void?**

The Psychology of "Showing Off"

There's no denying that some wealthy individuals enjoy flaunting their success through branded goods. This is what psychologists refer to as **conspicuous consumption** — the act of buying and displaying expensive items to signal wealth and status. But behind this behavior lies a more complex set of motivations.

At its core, conspicuous consumption is often driven by the need for **social validation.** Just as middle-class consumers may feel pressure to keep up with their peers by buying branded goods, the rich, too, feel a pressure to maintain their position at the top of the social hierarchy. In this way, branded goods become tools of social power — a way to signal superiority and command respect.

For individuals like Rohit, the act of purchasing luxury items isn't just about personal enjoyment — it's about **projecting success.** Whether it's at a business meeting, a wedding, or a social gathering, wearing a designer suit or driving an expensive car sends a message: "I have made it. I am successful."

But here's the irony: While branded goods can boost one's social standing in the eyes of others, they don't always bring personal fulfillment. Many wealthy individuals find themselves constantly chasing the next luxury purchase, hoping that it will bring them the happiness or contentment they seek. But just like for the middle class, this satisfaction is often short-lived.

The Thin Line Between Celebration and Flaunting

While some rich individuals may buy luxury goods to flaunt their wealth, others do so as a way of celebrating their achievements. For someone who has worked hard to build a successful business or career, buying a luxury car or a high-end watch can feel like a reward — a way to mark their success and enjoy the fruits of their labor.

Take the example of Alok, a self-made entrepreneur from Mumbai. After years of struggling to get his business off the ground, Alok finally achieved financial success. To celebrate, he bought himself a luxury car, not to show off to others, but because it represented a personal milestone. For him, the car wasn't just a status symbol — it was a symbol of his hard work, perseverance, and achievement.

This is where the line between celebration and flaunting becomes blurred. For some, buying luxury goods is about personal enjoyment and celebrating their success. For others, it's about signaling their status to the world. And in many cases, it's a mix of both.

But what happens when the desire to celebrate turns into a need for validation? When the act of buying branded goods shifts from being a reward to becoming a way to maintain one's social image?

The Social Pressure of Wealth: Keeping Up Appearances

It's easy to assume that the wealthy are immune to social pressure, but in reality, they often face their own unique set of challenges. For many rich individuals, maintaining their social image requires constant effort. Whether it's attending high-profile events, being part of elite social circles, or owning the latest luxury items, the pressure to keep up appearances is ever-present.

For example, in affluent neighborhoods like South Delhi or Mumbai's Pali Hill, there's often an unspoken competition among the wealthy to outdo one another. Whether it's upgrading to a bigger house, buying a more expensive car, or throwing lavish parties, the pressure to maintain one's status can lead to **excessive consumption.**

Rohit, for instance, bought things he didn't really need, simply because he felt the pressure to keep up with his wealthy peers. If a friend upgraded to a more luxurious car, Rohit felt compelled to do the same. If a colleague bought an expensive watch, Rohit would start browsing for one too. It became less about personal desire and more about **keeping up with the social elite.**

This pressure can create a cycle of **social comparison**, where individuals are constantly measuring their success against others. And for the rich, this often means buying more and more expensive items to stay at the top of the social ladder. But the question is: Does this constant comparison bring genuine happiness, or does it lead to stress, dissatisfaction, and a never-ending quest for more?

Do We Really Need It, or Do We Just Want It?

For both the rich and the middle class, there's a critical question that one must ask before every luxury purchase: **Do we really need it, or do we just want it?**

For many wealthy individuals, the line between need and want becomes blurred. When you have the financial means to buy whatever you desire, it's easy to convince yourself that every purchase is justified. But as we've seen, the satisfaction that comes from branded goods is often fleeting. The excitement of owning a new luxury item fades quickly, and what remains is often a feeling of emptiness or dissatisfaction.

This is why it's important to recognize that **branded goods, no matter how expensive, cannot fill emotional voids.** They may provide temporary excitement or social validation, but they cannot bring lasting fulfillment or inner peace. True contentment comes not from what we own, but from how we live our lives.

Conclusion: Beyond the Need to Show Off

For the rich, buying branded goods is often about more than just owning expensive items — it's about projecting success, commanding respect, and maintaining social status. But the key to finding true happiness isn't in showing off wealth; it's in recognizing that material possessions, no matter how luxurious, cannot bring lasting fulfillment.

Rohit eventually realized this after years of chasing after branded goods. While his possessions impressed others, they didn't bring him the inner peace he was searching for. Over time, he began shifting his focus from material success to personal growth, investing in experiences, relationships, and self-improvement.

At the end of the day, the rich, like everyone else, must ask themselves: Are we buying these things to bring joy into our lives, or are we just trying to impress others? The answer can make all the difference.

End of Part II: History and Human Nature – The Desire for Superiority

Part II explored the historical and cultural roots of luxury, revealing that the desire to display wealth is deeply ingrained in human nature. We looked at how this drive for superiority and social distinction has shaped consumer behavior for centuries. Key takeaways are:

1. **The Middle-Class Dilemma**: The middle class often feels caught between aspirations for luxury and financial reality, leading to internal conflict and frustration.

2. **Influence of Media and Influencers**: Media and influencers play a pivotal role in shaping consumer aspirations, normalizing luxury consumption as a marker of success and desirability.

3. **The Desire for Superiority**: From ancient royalty to modern consumers, people have used material displays to signify status and superiority, highlighting a timeless aspect of human nature.

PART III

ECONOMIC AND MARKET DYNAMICS OF LUXURY

Chapter 7

Are Branded Goods a Necessity or Just a Desire?

When Meera bought her first pair of luxury shoes, she felt like she had finally arrived. She had seen countless influencers and celebrities flaunting similar pairs on social media, and now it was her turn. But after a few weeks, the excitement faded. The shoes, though beautiful, were just shoes. They didn't change her life or make her feel any more successful than before. She began to wonder: were branded goods something she really needed, or were they just a desire she had built up in her mind?

In a world where branded goods are marketed as necessities — symbols of success, sophistication, and achievement — it's easy to get caught up in the idea that owning these items is essential. But do we really need branded goods to feel complete, or are they simply desires created by clever marketing?

In this chapter, we will explore the difference between **need** and **desire** for branded goods, and how recognizing this distinction can help us make more mindful choices about what we buy.

The Illusion of Necessity: How Brands Create Demand

At its core, branding is about creating desire. Luxury brands spend millions of dollars every year to convince consumers that their products are not just desirable, but essential. Whether it's through celebrity endorsements, high-budget advertising campaigns, or influencer partnerships, brands know how to tap into the human desire for success, validation, and belonging.

Take the example of branded smartphones. Every year, companies release newer models with incremental upgrades — a slightly better camera, a faster processor, or a new design. But are these features really necessary? For most consumers, the previous model works perfectly fine. Yet, the marketing campaigns surrounding new releases make it seem like the older models are suddenly outdated, and consumers feel the pressure to upgrade.

This is what's known as **artificial demand** — the perception that a product is a necessity, even when it isn't. For brands, creating artificial demand is key to driving sales. By convincing consumers that their lives will be incomplete without the latest product, brands manage to transform desire into a perceived need.

Do Branded Goods Really Improve Our Lives?

One of the key questions to ask when considering a branded purchase is: **Will this item actually improve my life?**

For some products, the answer might be yes. Branded items often come with higher quality, better craftsmanship, and longer-lasting materials. For example, a well-made pair of branded shoes might last longer and be more comfortable than a cheaper alternative. Similarly, luxury electronics might offer better features or more reliable performance than lower-end models.

However, for many branded goods, the improvements they offer are often marginal — or even non-existent. Take designer clothes, for instance. While they might offer a higher quality of fabric or a more flattering fit, they often come with a price tag that far exceeds their practical value. What we're really paying for, in many cases, is the **brand name**, not the utility of the product.

Meera realized this after her luxury shoe purchase. While the shoes were well made, she could have easily found a similar pair at a fraction of the price, without sacrificing comfort or style. In the end, the purchase was more about the perceived value of the brand than the actual need for the shoes.

The Role of Social Status in Shaping Perceived Needs

In India, social status plays a significant role in shaping consumer behavior. For many middle-class individuals, branded goods are seen as a way to signal upward mobility and success. This is particularly true in a country where economic disparities are stark, and where owning luxury items is seen as a marker of having "arrived" in life.

For instance, think about the social significance of owning a luxury car. In many parts of urban India, driving a high-end vehicle is not just about transportation — it's about making a statement. The car becomes a symbol of success, a way of showing the world that you have achieved a certain level of wealth and social standing.

But here's the question: **Do these symbols of success actually bring happiness, or do they create more pressure?** For many middle-class individuals, the pressure to maintain this image can lead to financial strain, as they take on debt or stretch their budgets to buy luxury items they don't really need.

Suresh, a small business owner in Hyderabad, learned this lesson the hard way. After years of hard work, he finally saved enough to buy a luxury car. But soon after making the purchase, he realized that the car didn't bring him the satisfaction he expected. Instead, it brought financial stress, as the monthly payments ate into his savings. What was once a symbol of success quickly became a burden.

Needs vs. Wants: Recognizing the Difference

One of the biggest challenges consumer faces is distinguishing between **needs** and **wants**. In today's consumer-driven society, it's easy to convince ourselves that we need things we don't. But understanding the difference between these two can help us make more mindful decisions about what we buy.

Here's a simple way to break it down:

- **Needs** are items or services that are essential for our well-being, safety, and survival. This includes basic necessities like food, clothing, shelter, and healthcare. For luxury goods, certain items might improve our quality of life, but they are rarely essential.

- **Wants** are items or services that bring us pleasure, enjoyment, or social status, but are not necessary for our well-being. Branded goods, in most cases, fall into this category. While they might make us feel good or enhance our social standing, they are not essential for our day-to-day survival.

Once we recognize that many of the branded goods we desire are wants, not needs, we can start making more thoughtful choices about where to allocate our money. This doesn't mean we should never indulge in luxury items, but it does mean being more intentional about our purchases and asking ourselves whether they align with our long-term goals and values.

Breaking Free from the Illusion of Necessity

If you find yourself constantly chasing after branded goods, it's important to take a step back and reflect on why. Are you buying these items because you genuinely need them, or because you've been conditioned to believe that they are essential for happiness and success?

Here are a few strategies to help break free from the illusion of necessity:

1. **Pause Before You Purchase:** Before making a branded purchase, take a moment to reflect on whether the item is a need or a want. Ask yourself if it will truly improve your life, or if you're buying it to keep up with others, or to seek validation.

2. **Focus on Quality, Not Brands:** Sometimes, it's worth investing in high-quality items, but this doesn't always mean buying from a luxury brand. Look for products that offer durability, functionality, and craftsmanship, rather than simply focusing on the brand name.

3. **Set Clear Priorities:** Align your spending with your values. If financial security, personal growth, or experiences are more important to you than owning luxury items, prioritize your spending in those areas. Remember, branded goods can bring temporary happiness, but they won't solve deeper emotional needs.

4. **Challenge the Status Quo:** Don't be afraid to question societal norms around consumption. Just because others are buying luxury goods doesn't mean you have to. Choose what works best for your life, not what others expect of you.

Conclusion: Rethinking Necessity

The question isn't whether branded goods are bad or good — it's about understanding why we desire them and whether they truly bring value to our lives. For Meera, the realization that her luxury shoes were a want, not a need, helped her shift her focus toward more meaningful purchases. Instead of chasing after the next branded item, she started prioritizing experiences, savings, and personal growth.

By rethinking our approach to consumption and recognizing the difference between needs and desires, we can make more conscious, fulfilling choices that align with our true values. Branded goods might be tempting, but true contentment comes from living authentically and mindfully.

Lessons from Kings, Queens, and Aristocracy: Historical Insights on Wealth Display

Throughout history, the desire to display wealth and superiority has been a defining feature of humanity. From the opulent palaces of

Indian maharajas to the grand courts of European kings and queens, luxury has always been a symbol of power, influence, and status. In ancient times, the grandeur of a ruler's possessions — their gold-laden crowns, extravagant garments, and treasure-filled palaces — wasn't just about personal indulgence. It was a way to assert dominance, command respect, and create a sense of awe among their subjects.

But as times changed, this show of wealth didn't disappear. Today, branded goods and luxury items serve a similar function for the modern aristocracy — the wealthy elite. Though we no longer live in a world of monarchs ruling kingdoms, the desire to signal superiority through material possessions has remained a constant part of human nature.

In this chapter, we will explore how the patterns of luxury consumption seen in ancient kings and queens have trickled down to modern society, influencing the way we think about wealth, power, and superiority. We'll look at the parallels between ancient royalty and today's wealthy elite and how the middle class often gets trapped in the same mindset.

Luxury as a Symbol of Power in Ancient Times

In ancient India, kings and queens ruled not just through military strength, but through their ability to project power. One of the most visible ways they did this was through their opulence. Whether it was the grandeur of their palaces, the richness of their attire, or the jewels they adorned themselves with, luxury was a way to communicate their dominance over others.

Take, for example, the Mughal emperors of India. They adorned their palaces with gold, precious stones, and intricate artwork. Their courts were filled with the finest silk garments, Persian rugs, and jewel-encrusted furniture. These displays of wealth weren't just for personal pleasure — they were designed to impress foreign dignitaries, intimidate rivals, and assert the emperor's divine right to rule.

Similarly, in European monarchies, kings and queens wore crowns encrusted with diamonds, rubies, and sapphires. The grand ceremonies, the lavish banquets, and the processions through city streets all served to reinforce the idea that the ruler was superior to the common man.

But beneath all this grandeur lay a deeper message: **wealth equals' power**. The more extravagant the ruler's possessions, the greater their perceived strength. And this message wasn't just for the elite — it was also for the masses, who looked up to their rulers as symbols of authority and influence.

How Modern Aristocrats Display Their Wealth

Today, we no longer live in a world where kings and queens rule over empires. But the desire to display wealth and power is as strong as ever. For the modern elite — the CEOs, celebrities, and business tycoons — branded goods and luxury items serve a similar purpose as the gold crowns and palaces of ancient rulers.

Think about the modern-day equivalent of a royal procession. In cities like Mumbai and Delhi, luxury cars and high-end SUVs often signal the arrival of someone important. The branded clothing, the designer jewelry, and the extravagant homes all serve as markers of success and influence. For the wealthy elite, these possessions are not just about personal enjoyment — they are about **social signaling**.

For instance, owning a luxury car in India is more than just about transportation. It's a way to signal to others that you've "made it." Whether it's pulling up to a five-star hotel or attending a high-profile event, the car you drive speaks volumes about your status. Similarly, wearing a luxury watch or carrying a designer handbag isn't just about functionality — it's about sending a message to those around you.

But here's the critical difference between ancient rulers and today's wealthy elite: **accessibility**. While kings and queens were born into their positions of power, today's wealthy often earn their status through business, innovation, or celebrity. This means that wealth is no longer confined to a select few — it's attainable (at least in theory) for anyone willing to work hard enough. But with this accessibility comes a new challenge: the pressure to keep up.

The Middle-Class Trap: Aspiring to Aristocracy

The desire to display wealth hasn't just affected the rich. For many middle-class individuals, the **aspiration to live like the wealthy** creates a constant cycle of consumption. The same principles that guided ancient kings and queens — the need to display superiority, to be admired, and to command respect — are now driving modern consumers to seek branded goods and luxury items.

This is true in India, where the cultural significance of wealth and status is deeply ingrained. In a society where social hierarchies are still prevalent, owning luxury goods is often seen as a way to signal upward mobility. For many middle-class families, branded goods are not just a personal indulgence — they are a way to demonstrate that they've "arrived."

Take the example of Shalini, a middle-class housewife in Bengaluru. When she bought her first designer saree, it wasn't just about wearing something beautiful. It was about being seen at weddings and family functions as someone who could afford luxury. Her saree wasn't just an outfit — it was a statement. But the more Shalini bought into this mindset, the more she felt the pressure to keep buying. Each family event became an opportunity to showcase her wealth, and soon, her closet was filled with designer clothes that she rarely wore.

For people like Shalini, the aspiration to live like the wealthy creates a financial and emotional burden. The desire to fit in, to be admired, and to project success often leads to **overconsumption** and **financial**

strain. And just like ancient kings and queens, the middle class finds itself trapped in a cycle of displaying wealth to maintain social standing.

Human Nature and the Desire for Superiority

At its core, human nature drives the desire to display wealth. From ancient times to the modern era, people have always sought ways to demonstrate their superiority over others. Whether it's through possessions, titles, or achievements, humans are driven by the need to be seen as successful, powerful, and influential.

But here's the problem: **superiority is a moving target**. No matter how much wealth we accumulate or how many branded goods we own, there will always be someone with more. This creates a never-ending cycle of competition, where the goalposts keep shifting, and the desire for more never fully goes away.

For the working-class, this desire for superiority often leads to misunderstanding between aspirations and reality. While branded goods might offer a temporary sense of success, they don't bring lasting fulfillment. Instead, they create a constant need for validation — a need that can only be satisfied by the next purchase.

Learning from History: The Cost of Excess

While kings and queens may have enjoyed the luxuries of their time, their excesses often came at a cost. Throughout history, many monarchies fell because of their extravagance, leaving behind bankrupt treasuries and discontented populations. The lesson is obvious: **excessive consumption is unsustainable.**

For the middle class today, the lesson is just as relevant. The pursuit of branded goods and luxury items may bring temporary satisfaction, but in the long run, it can lead to financial instability, emotional stress, and a sense of emptiness. Just like the fall of ancient empires, the constant chase for more can leave us feeling depleted and unfulfilled.

Conclusion: Rethinking Modern-Day Aristocracy

The desire to display wealth and superiority has been a part of human history for centuries. But while ancient kings and queens may have had the means to live in luxury, the middle class today time and again finds itself stretched thin by the pressures of consumerism.

By recognizing the patterns of excess and overconsumption that have played out through history, we can begin to rethink our own approach to wealth and status. Instead of chasing after branded goods as symbols of success, we can choose to focus on what truly matters: personal fulfillment, meaningful relationships, and financial stability.

Shalini, after years of buying into the mindset of aristocracy, eventually realized that her designer sarees didn't bring her the happiness she was seeking. She shifted her focus away from material possessions and started investing in experiences that enriched her life. In doing so, she found a sense of peace that no amount of luxury goods could provide.

End of Part III: Economic and Market Dynamics of Luxury

In Part III, we focused on the economic forces that drive the luxury market and influence consumer behavior. From scarcity marketing to the aspirational allure of luxury goods, this part delved into how the industry sustains itself by appealing to consumer psychology. Key takeaways include:

1. **Desire Over Necessity**: While not essential items, luxury goods are marketed in a way that instills a strong desire to own them, especially among aspirational consumers.
2. **Middle-Class Confusion**: The middle class often finds itself in a cycle of spending on luxury items to emulate wealthier individuals, which can lead to financial strain.
3. **Historical Lessons**: The use of luxury as a symbol of power and status has historical roots, showing that material displays of wealth have long been a part of society's fabric.

PART IV

THE ETHICAL AND PSYCHOLOGICAL TRAP OF LUXURY GOODS

Chapter 9

Walking Billboards – The Indian Love Affair with Brands

In the bustling streets of India's urban landscapes, there's one sight you can't miss — individuals proudly strutting in luxury branded items from head to toe, as if they're walking advertisements for the world's most elite brands. From high-end shopping districts to neighborhood cafes, the obsession with flaunting branded shoes, belts, clothes, and accessories is an everyday phenomenon. The most striking aspect is how people treat these luxury goods as status symbols, often creating an image that's more of a walking boutique than a personal style statement.

Picture this: a young man strolling through the local high street, his gleaming white **Balenciaga** sneakers catching the light, while his **Hermès** belt, with its signature 'H' buckle, commands attention. His **Burberry** trench coat drapes perfectly over his **Dior** shirt, the logo positioned just right for passersby to notice. It's hard not to see the effort he's putting into his ensemble, ensuring each brand is displayed like a badge of honor. Is he comfortable? Hardly. His walk feels more like a performance, a deliberate act to flaunt his curated luxury items. Every step he takes is a calculated attempt to showcase the brands he's wearing — as if each logo solidifies his place in society.

Across the street, a woman with an oversized **Chanel** tote maneuvers through a supermarket, her **Cartier** bracelet glinting under the fluorescent lights as she pushes her shopping cart. She's wearing a pair of sleek **Louboutin** heels and an iconic **Balmain** blazer. Her appearance screams high fashion, but in the setting of a grocery store, it almost feels surreal. She's more prepared for a fashion shoot than a weekend errand. The contrast between her attire and her surroundings creates an unintentionally comical scene, one that doesn't go unnoticed by onlookers who smile at the extravagance of it all.

This spectacle isn't confined to the ultra-elite. Even in middle-class neighborhoods, you'll find individuals who have saved for months to afford that one luxury item. Perhaps a pair of **Ray-Ban** aviators or a **Louis Vuitton** wallet — each of these pieces becomes a symbol of success, a way to announce to the world, "I've made it." But often, the reality doesn't match the perception. The person proudly showing off their **Gucci** sneakers may have spent months saving for them, or worse, incurred debt to own them, believing that these branded goods elevate their social status.

What's most striking, and often humorous, is the deliberate effort to display these brands. Simply wearing a **Rolex** isn't enough; The branded shoes aren't just worn; they're shown off with deliberate movements, ensuring the logos are visible with every step. It's as if these individuals have signed an invisible contract to be walking billboards for luxury brands, yet without of the financial compensation that a real advertisement would provide.

This phenomenon has created a curious reality where the obsession with luxury goods has led people to focus less on personal comfort and style and more on external validation. It's not about how the clothes feel or even how they look on the person — it's about ensuring that the world knows they're wearing **Tom Ford** sunglasses or a Yves **Saint Laurent** jacket. The more prominent the logo, the more successful they appear, or so they believe.

It's not unusual to see entire groups of friends dressed in head-to-toe designer outfits, each trying to subtly outdo the other in a friendly yet competitive showcase of luxury. One friend might sport a **Bottega Veneta** handbag, while other shows off a **Fendi** scarf. Social gatherings transform into informal fashion parades where the conversation revolves less around meaningful connections and more around comparisons of who's wearing what. The unspoken contest of "keeping up with the brands" is alive and well.

But the irony here is that, while these individuals believe they're exuding sophistication and class, many observers can't help but chuckle at the scene. Instead of looking polished or stylish, they sometimes come across as over-the-top or ostentatious. It's a paradox — what's intended as a display of wealth and taste often turns into something that borders on caricature. The logos become louder than the individual wearing them, reducing their personal style to a series of labels.

However, this brand obsession has a darker side, especially for the middle class. Many find themselves trapped in a cycle of aspiration, where owning these luxury items becomes more than just a fashion choice — it's seen as a symbol of personal worth.

At the heart of this behavior lies a fundamental question: Are we purchasing luxury goods because they genuinely make us happy, or are we buying them to show the world that we've "made it"? When individuals start resembling walking brand shops, it's time to reflect on what luxury truly means. Are we chasing happiness, or just chasing logos?

The allure of luxury is strong, and in small doses, it can bring joy. But when we lose ourselves in the pursuit of branded goods, we risk turning our identity into a collection of labels, sacrificing comfort, individuality, and even financial stability. In the end, we must ask ourselves if the cost of this luxury is truly worth it — not just in rupees or dollars, but in how much of our sense of self we hand over to these global brands.

Chapter 10

The Economics of Luxury – How Markets Shape Our Desires

Luxury goods are not just about beautiful designs, impeccable craftsmanship, or prestigious brand names. They're about economics. Every branded product you see in high-end malls or on celebrities' Instagram feeds is part of a carefully orchestrated market that plays on human psychology. These goods are made scarce, exclusive, and aspirational — driving up their value and, ultimately, their price. But have you ever wondered how the economics of luxury works? How do brands convince us that their products are worth 10 times more than non-branded alternatives?

In this chapter, we'll explore the economic forces behind luxury goods — from the **scarcity principle** to the **artificial inflation of value** — and how these tactics play into the desires of both the rich and the middle class. We'll also take a closer look at the market dynamics that make luxury goods seem like necessities and how brands manipulate consumer behavior to fuel this demand.

The Scarcity Principle: Why Less Means More

One of the most powerful strategies that luxury brands use to increase demand is the **scarcity principle**. This is the idea that the rarer something is, the more valuable it becomes. From limited-edition handbags to exclusive luxury car models, brands often create an artificial sense of scarcity to drive up the perceived value of their products.

Consider a luxury watch company that only produces a few hundred watches in a particular design each year. Even though the company has the capacity to produce thousands of watches, they deliberately keep production low to maintain exclusivity. As a result, the watch becomes a coveted item — something that only a few people can own. This sense of rarity makes the product seem more desirable, even though the intrinsic value of the watch may not justify its price.

For the middle class, this scarcity can create a **fear of missing out**. If a product is presented as exclusive, consumers are more likely to desire it, simply because they perceive it to be scarce and unique.

This is especially true in India, where the desire to own something exclusive is tied to social status.

The Myth of Quality: Is It Really Worth the Price?

One of the key selling points of luxury brands is the idea that their products are of **superior quality**. While it's true that many luxury goods use high-quality materials and craftsmanship, the price difference between luxury and non-luxury items is often far greater than the actual difference in quality.

Take, for example, a high-end leather handbag. While the materials may be premium, the craftsmanship meticulous, and the design sophisticated, does that justify a price tag of ₹1,50,000 when a non-branded leather handbag with similar materials and design costs ₹5,000? The answer lies not in the product itself, but in the brand behind it. Consumers aren't just paying for the bag — they're paying for the **status** that comes with owning a luxury brand.

For many middle-class individuals, this creates a **psychological dilemma**. On one hand, they recognize that they're paying more for the brand name than the actual product. On the other hand, they want the prestige that comes with owning a luxury item. This tension between practicality and desire drives many middle-class consumers to stretch their budgets for branded goods.

The Role of Marketing in Creating Desire

If you've ever felt an overwhelming urge to buy a branded product, even though you didn't need it, you've experienced the power of **marketing**. Luxury brands are masters of creating desire through advertising, storytelling, and influencer partnerships. Every time you see a luxury item in a glossy magazine, on a billboard, or featured by a celebrity, you're being exposed to a carefully crafted image of success, elegance, and exclusivity.

Marketing creates the illusion that owning a luxury item will elevate your life. Whether it's a perfume that promises to make you feel more confident or a watch that symbolizes success, luxury brands tap into our emotional desires. They sell us not only products, but **lifestyles.**

For instance, a luxury car brand might advertise their latest model with images of the car speeding down an open road, with a successful-looking driver behind the wheel. The message is clear: If you own this car, you too will experience freedom, adventure, and success. It's not about the car's engine or features — it's about what the car represents.

This type of marketing is effective for the working class, who often aspire to achieve the lifestyles depicted in these ads. For someone who has worked hard to reach financial stability, the idea of owning a luxury item can feel like a **reward** for their efforts. But more often than not, this desire roots from marketing manipulation rather than genuine need.

Artificial Inflation: How Brands Control Prices

Another economic factor that drives the luxury market is **artificial inflation.** Luxury brands deliberately keep prices high to maintain the exclusivity and desirability of their products. The cost of producing a luxury item is far lower than its retail price. But by positioning the product as expensive, the brand can create a sense of prestige around it.

For example, a luxury fashion brand might charge ₹50,000 for a pair of sunglasses that cost ₹5,000 to produce. The high price isn't necessarily a reflection of the materials or craftsmanship — it's a reflection of the brand's **strategy** to maintain its elite image. By keeping prices high, the brand ensures that only a select few can afford their products, reinforcing the idea that owning the item is a mark of success.

This pricing strategy also appeals to the middle class. When a product is expensive, it's often perceived as more valuable. Many middle-class consumers believe that by saving up for a luxury item, they are buying into a world of superior quality and exclusivity. But in reality, they are often paying for **perception**, not **performance**.

The Role of Upscale Market Platforms

In recent years, the rise of upscale market platforms has made luxury goods more accessible to the middle class. Online marketplaces like Amazon's luxury section, Tata CLiQ Luxury, Myntra Luxe and other high-end department stores have brought branded goods to a broader audience. While these platforms create more opportunities for middle-class consumers to purchase luxury items, they also create a new set of challenges.

On one hand, these platforms offer **convenience**. Consumers no longer have to visit exclusive boutiques to buy luxury goods — they can now shop online, browse through thousands of products, and have them delivered to their doorstep. This accessibility has made luxury more attainable for the average consumer.

This accessibility comes with a **psychological cost**. The more accessible luxury becomes, the more middle-class consumers feel the pressure to keep up with the latest trends. The ease of online shopping, combined with aggressive marketing and discounts, makes it tempting to buy branded goods that might not fit within one's budget.

For instance, Ramesh, a sales manager from Chennai, often browsed upscale platforms online, looking for deals on luxury watches. One day, he saw a branded watch he had always wanted on sale. Even though the discounted price was still beyond his budget, the "limited time offer" convinced him to make the purchase. While Ramesh felt a sense of satisfaction when he received the watch, the financial strain of the purchase weighed on him for months.

How Markets Exploit Human Nature

At the heart of the luxury market is a fundamental understanding of **human nature.** Brands are aware that the consumers are driven by desires for status, success, and belonging. By playing on these emotions, they create an environment where branded goods feel like essential markers of personal achievement.

For the working class, this can be particularly damaging. Many middle-class families aspire to reach a higher social status, and luxury goods seem like a shortcut to achieving that. But in reality, the pursuit of luxury often leads to financial stress, debt, and emotional dissatisfaction.

The market exploits this desire for more by offering a constant stream of new products, limited editions, and exclusive collaborations. The message is clear: if you don't keep up, you'll fall behind. But this message is a trap, designed to keep consumers in a cycle of consumption.

Breaking Free from Market Manipulation

If you've ever felt manipulated by luxury brands or pressured to buy something you didn't need, you're not alone. The luxury market is designed to make you feel this way. But by understanding the economic forces at play, you can start to take control of your purchasing decisions and make more conscious choices.

Here are a few strategies to help break free from market manipulation:

1. **Be Aware of Marketing Tactics:** Recognize that many luxury ads are designed to appeal to your emotions, not your needs. Before

making a purchase, ask yourself if you truly need the item or if you're being influenced by the lifestyle depicted in the ad.

2. **Don't Fall for Scarcity Tactics:** Just because a product is labeled as "limited edition" doesn't mean you need it. Luxury brands often create artificial scarcity to drive demand. Take your time to consider if the product is worth the price, or if you're just feeling pressured to buy it before it's gone.

3. **Focus on Value, Not Price:** Remember that high prices don't always equal high quality. Look for products that offer genuine value — whether that's in terms of durability, functionality, or personal significance — rather than simply buying for the brand name.

4. **Set Boundaries for Online Shopping:** Upscale market platforms can make luxury goods feel more accessible, but they can also encourage impulse purchases. Set a budget for luxury spending and avoid buying items that don't align with your financial goals.

Conclusion: Understanding the Economics of Desire

The luxury market is a complex system designed to create desire, drive demand, and inflate value. By understanding how these economic forces work, we can start to see through the tactics used by luxury brands to manipulate our desires. For the economy class, this knowledge is crucial. While the temptation to own branded goods is strong, it's important to recognize that much of what we perceive as necessity is, in fact, carefully crafted marketing and economic strategy.

Luxury goods can bring temporary satisfaction, but they rarely provide lasting fulfillment. The constant push to keep up with trends, to own the latest limited-edition product, or to fit into a certain social circle often leads to stress and financial strain rather than happiness.

By taking a step back and analyzing the economic forces at play, we can start making mindful decisions about where and how we spend our money. Whether it's questioning the true value of a luxury item or resisting the pressure to buy into exclusivity, the key is to focus on what truly brings value and meaning to our lives.

Chapter 11

The Pros of Branded Goods – When Luxury Makes Sense

Luxury and branded goods often get criticized for being unnecessary or indulgent, but they can also offer genuine value when used wisely. While it's easy to dismiss expensive items as purely status symbols, there are times when investing in a high-quality, branded product can be a smart decision. Whether it's the durability, craftsmanship, or the psychological satisfaction that comes from owning something you've earned, branded goods can have their advantages.

In this chapter, we will explore the **positive side of branded goods**, examining when luxury items make sense and how they can enhance life in practical, emotional, and even financial ways. We'll also look at how to balance the appeal of luxury with responsible spending, ensuring that purchases bring real value rather than just temporary satisfaction.

Quality and Durability: When You Get What You Pay For

One of the key advantages of many branded goods is their **superior quality** and **durability**. High-end products, unlike cheaper alternatives, are made with better materials, more precise craftsmanship, and receive greater attention to detail. This means that they are likely to last longer, perform better, and offer more comfort or utility over time.

For instance, consider a branded leather handbag. While a non-branded alternative might look similar on the surface, the branded version is likely made from high-quality leather, stitched with stronger threads, and designed to withstand wear and tear. Here, the branded item is more than just a luxury — it's an investment in something that will last for years, if not decades.

This is especially true for items like **shoes, watches**, and **electronics**, where quality can directly affect performance and longevity. A well-made pair of shoes, for example, may be expensive upfront but could last years longer than a cheaper pair that needs to be replaced more frequently. In the long run, investing in quality can actually save money.

Emotional Satisfaction: The Joy of Ownership

Another often overlooked benefit of branded goods is the **emotional satisfaction** they provide. For many people, owning a luxury item can be a deeply rewarding experience. It can represent a personal achievement, a reward for hard work, or simply the joy of having something special that brings a sense of pride and confidence.

Take Priya, a 34-year-old architect in Mumbai. After completing a major project, she rewarded herself with a designer watch she had been eyeing for years. For Priya, the watch wasn't just about timekeeping — it was a symbol of her success and the long hours she had put into her career. Every time she wore the watch, it reminded her of her accomplishments and gave her a sense of satisfaction.

While emotional satisfaction is often criticized as being superficial, many people find that luxury items hold deep personal meaning for them. Whether it's a special piece of jewelry, a designer dress for a milestone event, or a luxury car that represents years of hard work, these items can bring joy and fulfillment beyond their practical use.

Investment Potential: When Luxury Goods Appreciate in Value

While most products lose value over time, some luxury items can actually **appreciate** in value, making them sound investments. This is particularly true for **collectible items** such as high-end watches, rare handbags, and certain pieces of jewelry or art. In some cases, owning a luxury item can be more than just a purchase — it can be a financial investment that grows in value over time.

For example, certain **luxury watches** from brands like Rolex or Patek Philippe are known to increase in value, especially if they are rare editions. Similarly, handbags from brands like Hermès or Chanel are considered collectibles, and their value can rise significantly on the resale market in some instances.

However, it's important to note that not all luxury items appreciate in value. The key is to do your research and invest in items that are known for their long-term value. For those who are savvy about luxury markets, owning certain branded goods can be a way to diversify their investment portfolio and potentially earn a return on their purchases.

Branded Goods as Symbols of Legacy

For many families, branded goods can also serve as **heirlooms** — items that are passed down from generation to generation, carrying with them stories, memories, and family history. Whether it's a piece of fine jewelry, a luxury watch, or a classic handbag, these items often take on emotional significance, as they are inherited by children or grandchildren.

Take, for example, Mehul, a businessman in Delhi, who inherited a vintage watch from his father. The watch wasn't just a valuable item — it represented his father's legacy, a reminder of the hard work and success his family had built over decades. Mehul didn't wear the watch often, but every time he did, it connected him to his family's history and the lessons his father had passed down.

In this sense, branded goods can serve as **symbols of continuity** and **family pride**, becoming cherished possessions that carry meaning beyond their monetary value. While luxury items might seem like indulgent purchases, they can also become lasting symbols of personal or family milestones, creating memories that endure for generations.

The Psychological Benefits of Ownership

For many people, owning a luxury item can boost their **self-esteem** and **confidence**. Whether it's wearing a designer outfit to a job interview or driving a high-end car to an important meeting, branded goods can provide a sense of empowerment and self-assurance. This boost in confidence can even translate into real-world success, as people feel more accomplished when they present themselves well.

Consider Anisha, a corporate executive in Bengaluru. After her company promoted her to a senior role, Anisha invested in a tailored designer suit for her first board meeting. While the suit was expensive, it made her feel confident and ready to tackle the challenges of her new position. The psychological impact of wearing something that made her feel powerful was worth the price tag.

While confidence shouldn't be tied solely to material possessions, there's no denying that certain branded items can provide a psychological boost. When used wisely, luxury goods can help people feel more confident and assertive, particularly in professional or social settings where appearance matters.

Balancing Luxury with Financial Responsibility

Of course, it's important to remember that luxury goods should never come at the expense of financial stability. While branded items can provide real value in certain situations, they should be purchased within the framework of responsible spending. The key is to strike a **balance** between enjoying the finer things in life and ensuring that your financial goals are met.

Here are a few tips for making luxury purchases without sacrificing financial health:

1. **Set Clear Financial Goals:** Before making a luxury purchase, ensure that you've met your financial priorities, such as savings, retirement, and emergency funds. Once these goals are secure, you can consider using a portion of your discretionary income for branded goods.
2. **Save for Big Purchases:** Instead of impulsively buying luxury items, take the time to save for them. This not only helps you

avoid debt, but also makes the purchase feel more rewarding once you've achieved it.

3. **Buy for Longevity:** When purchasing luxury goods, focus on items that will last. High-quality, timeless pieces are often better investments than trendy items that will go out of style quickly.

4. **Be Selective:** Not every branded item is worth the price. Choose luxury goods that hold personal significance, offer quality, or have potential long-term value. Avoid buying for the sake of social status alone.

Conclusion: When Luxury Adds Value

While it's easy to view branded goods as indulgent or unnecessary they can provide real value in certain circumstances. Whether it's through superior quality, emotional satisfaction, investment potential, or psychological benefits, luxury items can enhance life when approached mindfully.

For people like Priya, Anisha, or Mehul, luxury purchases weren't about showing off — they were about celebrating personal achievements, investing in long-lasting quality, and creating meaningful symbols of legacy. By balancing the desire for luxury with financial responsibility, it's possible to enjoy the pros of branded goods without falling into the trap of overconsumption.

Chapter 12

How Brands Exploit Human Hunger for Superiority

Humans have always had a natural drive for **status** and **superiority** — the need to stand out, be recognized, and feel valued by others. From ancient times, when kings and emperors used wealth to display power, to the modern world where branded goods serve as status symbols, the desire for superiority has shaped societies and economies. Luxury brands understand this instinct better than anyone, and they've mastered the art of exploiting it.

In this chapter, we will explore how brands tap into our **innate desire for superiority**, leveraging psychological tricks, social hierarchies, and marketing strategies to convince us that owning their products will elevate us in the eyes of others. We will also examine the effects of this exploitation on the middle class, who are often caught in the cycle of buying to feel superior, only to find themselves more stressed and financially strained in the process.

The Psychology of Superiority: Why We Want to Stand Out

From a young age, humans are conditioned to seek approval and validation. In childhood, we want to be the fastest runner or the smartest student in the class. As we grow older, these desires don't disappear — they simply evolve. Instead of trophies or grades, we start seeking validation through material possessions: clothes, cars, gadgets, and more. Luxury brands understand this fundamental aspect of human psychology and use it to create a **sense of exclusivity** around their products.

Consider how branded goods are positioned in the market. High-end brands don't just sell products; they sell **status**. A luxury car isn't just about transportation — it's about letting the world know you've made it. A designer handbag isn't just about functionality — it's about showing that you belong to a higher social class. The message is simple: owning these goods will make you superior to others.

This is particularly true in India, where social hierarchies are deeply ingrained in the culture. Owning branded goods is often seen as a way to rise above one's peers, to be recognized as successful, and important.

But this desire for superiority isn't just about materialism — it's about the **emotional validation** that comes with it.

How Brands Create a Sense of Exclusivity

One of the most effective ways brands exploit the hunger for superiority is by creating a sense of **exclusivity**. Luxury brands deliberately position themselves as accessible only to a select few, making their products seem more desirable simply because they are difficult to obtain.

For example, consider the limited-edition collections released by high-end fashion houses. These items are produced in small quantities and are marketed as exclusive pieces that only a lucky few can own. This scarcity creates a sense of urgency, driving consumers to purchase the item not just because they need it, but because they want to be part of an exclusive group.

This strategy also applies to **premium pricing**. By setting their prices high, luxury brands create the perception that their products are more valuable. The higher the price, the more exclusive the item feels, and the more consumers associate it with status and superiority.

For the working class, this sense of exclusivity can be both alluring and damaging. While the desire to own something rare and prestigious is strong, it often leads to financial strain, as people stretch their budgets to buy items they can't truly afford. The result is a cycle of **aspirational consumption**, where the need to feel superior drives consumers to make purchases that ultimately leave them stressed and dissatisfied.

The Role of Social Comparison: Keeping Up with the Joneses

A key factor in why brands are able to exploit the hunger for superiority is **social comparison**. Humans have a natural tendency to compare themselves to others, and luxury brands fuel this by positioning their products as markers of social success. When we see our friends, neighbors, or colleagues owning branded goods, we begin to feel like we need to keep up.

This phenomenon is referred to as **"keeping up with the Joneses"** — the idea that we measure our success not by our own standards, but by the standards set by those around us. As we are constantly exposed to the curated lives of others, filled with luxury vacations, designer clothes, and expensive gadgets, social media has only amplified this effect,

For many economy-class families, the pressure to keep up can be overwhelming. Seeing friends buy luxury cars, post pictures of branded outfits, or flaunt their latest gadgets creates a sense of inadequacy. This drives people to make purchases they don't need or can't afford, simply to maintain social standing.

Consider the story of Vivek, a young professional in Bengaluru. He had saved up for years to buy a modest car, but after seeing his colleagues upgrading to luxury models, he felt compelled to do the same. Even though it meant taking out a loan, Vivek bought a high-end car to match the status of his peers. But after the initial excitement faded, he found himself burdened by monthly payments that stretched his finances thin.

The Illusion of Happiness: Does Superiority Bring Fulfillment?

One of the most insidious ways that brands exploit the hunger for superiority is by promising **happiness**. Advertisements often show people using branded goods and looking happier, more successful, and more fulfilled. The underlying message is that owning these items will not only make you superior, but it will also bring you joy and contentment.

However, the reality is quite different. Research shows that while material possessions can bring temporary happiness, the satisfaction fades quickly. This is because human beings quickly adapt to new acquisitions, a phenomenon known as **hedonic adaptation.** The luxury car, designer handbag, or branded watch that once brought excitement soon becomes just another part of daily life, and the need for something new arises again.

For the middle class, this creates a dangerous cycle of **perpetual dissatisfaction.** The more we chase after branded goods in the hopes of finding happiness, the more we realize that the happiness they bring is fleeting. This leads to more spending, more stress, and a constant feeling of not having enough.

How Brands Exploit Insecurity

Brands also tap into human **insecurities** to fuel the desire for superiority. Many luxury advertisements subtly imply that without their products, you are less than others. If you don't drive a luxury car, wear branded clothes, or own the latest gadget, you risk being seen as unsuccessful, unimportant, or even inferior.

This is effective in a country like India, where societal expectations and status symbols play a significant role in how people perceive themselves. In many cases, the desire to own branded goods isn't just about wanting to feel superior — it's about avoiding feelings of **inferiority.** The fear of being left behind or being seen as "less than" drives many middle-class families to spend beyond their means.

The Economic Impact of Superiority-Driven Consumption

While the desire for superiority drives consumption, it often has negative consequences for the middle class. The economic impact of trying to keep up with branded goods can be significant. Many families find themselves in debt, struggling to keep up with payments on luxury items they bought in pursuit of status.

This creates a **vicious cycle**: as people buy more branded goods to feel superior, they face financial strain, which leads to stress and dissatisfaction. This stress fuels the need to buy more in the hopes of finding happiness or maintaining social standing.

For the middle class, this cycle can be difficult to break. The economic pressure to keep up with branded goods can lead to long-term financial insecurity, with families sacrificing savings, investments, and even basic needs to maintain a façade of success.

Breaking Free from the Superiority Trap

The first step to breaking free from the superiority trap is to recognize the **psychological manipulation** at play. By understanding how brands exploit our desire for status and superiority, we can begin to make more conscious decisions about our purchases.

Here are a few strategies to help:

1. **Challenge the Idea of Superiority:** Ask yourself whether owning a branded item will truly make you feel superior or whether it's simply an illusion created by marketing. Remember that true superiority doesn't come from material possessions, but from personal fulfillment, relationships, and self-worth.
2. **Focus on What Brings Lasting Happiness:** Instead of seeking temporary satisfaction through branded goods, invest in experiences and relationships that bring long-term happiness. Studies show that experiences, such as travel, learning, and spending time with loved ones, bring more lasting joy than material possessions.
3. **Resist Social Comparison:** It's easy to fall into the trap of comparing yourself to others, especially in today's social media-

driven world. But remember that everyone's journey is different. Focus on your own goals and values, and resist the pressure to keep up with others' material possessions.

4. **Prioritize Financial Stability:** Ensure that your financial health comes first. Avoid going into debt or sacrificing savings for the sake of luxury goods. Financial freedom brings more peace of mind than any branded product ever could.

Conclusion: Reclaiming Control Over Our Desires

The hunger for superiority is a powerful force, and luxury brands have become experts at exploiting it. By tapping into our need for status, exclusivity, and validation, they convince us that owning branded goods will make us happier, more successful, and more fulfilled.

However, true fulfillment cannot be achieved through material possessions. It comes from living authentically, pursuing meaningful goals, and building strong relationships. By recognizing the psychological tricks used by brands and focusing on what truly matters, we can break free from the superiority trap and reclaim control over our desires.

Chapter 13

The Role of Culture and Tradition in Luxury Perception

In many cultures, including India's, the concept of luxury goes beyond personal taste—it's deeply rooted in tradition, heritage, and social identity. The idea of displaying wealth is woven into the fabric of cultural customs, where material items often symbolize prosperity, family pride, and even social standing. In this chapter, we'll explore how cultural values shape the perception of luxury and how traditional markers of status are evolving to include modern brands and goods. This cultural lens offers unique insight into why people purse branded items and how these desires are tied to deeper societal values.

---

1. Traditional Markers of Wealth: From Gold to Heirlooms

Historically, luxury in India has been tied to items like gold, silver, and other precious materials. Gold jewelry, for instance, has long symbolized family wealth and security. From weddings to religious events, gold is considered auspicious and serves as a testament to a family's prosperity. Heirloom jewelry and silk sarees, passed down through generations, carry not just material value but cultural and emotional significance, connecting families to their heritage.

Even in today's brand-centric world, these traditional markers of wealth still hold strong, especially during significant life events like weddings. Families invest heavily in gold, silver, and elaborate attire, seeing these as an enduring display of prosperity and respect for tradition. This blend of cultural values with luxury consumption shows that luxury isn't only about current trends but also about honoring one's lineage and cultural roots.

---

2. The Influence of Westernization and Globalization on Indian Luxury

As India has become more connected to global markets, the influence of Western brands and consumer culture has grown. Branded handbags, watches, and luxury cars have become symbols of modern success, and many young professionals now view these items as essential for projecting their status. The arrival of Western luxury brands in Indian cities has transformed the shopping landscape, offering people the chance to align with international symbols of success and sophistication.

This fusion of traditional values and Western luxury is unique. While families may still prioritize gold and heirlooms, there's a growing trend to incorporate high-end Western brands as a way of signaling modernity. For example, at Indian weddings, alongside traditional jewelry, you'll often see luxury watches and designer accessories as part of the bride's and groom's outfits. The blending of these symbols speaks to a dual identity—one that respects heritage while embracing global standards of luxury.

---

3. Social Pressure and the Concept of "Keeping Up"

In a society where social gatherings and festivals play a central role, the pressure to display wealth can be intense. Whether at weddings, festivals, or family functions, there's often an unspoken expectation to "keep up" with one's peers by showcasing luxury items. In this environment, owning branded goods isn't just a personal preference; it's a reflection of social standing and often a means of gaining respect within one's community.

For instance, consider the tradition of Diwali gifting. While this used to be a simple exchange of sweets and symbolic gifts, it has developed into a competition of luxury. Today, it's not uncommon to see people gifting designer items or premium gadgets as a way of demonstrating their generosity and wealth. This cultural practice highlights how luxury has intertwined with tradition, turning social customs into displays of affluence.

---

4. Modern Markers of Success: The Rise of Branded Goods

Today, items like designer handbags, luxury watches, and branded clothes have become status symbols in India, particularly among the urban middle class and affluent millennials. This shift reflects a broader change in values, where modern success is often measured by material acquisitions. The working class, in particular, finds itself navigating a space between traditional expectations and modern aspirations, often choosing branded goods to signal achievement and progress.

Brands like Louis Vuitton, Gucci, and Rolex have come to represent not only personal success but also social mobility. For some, owning these items serves as a testament to their hard work and economic advancement. By integrating branded goods into their lives, people often feel they're connecting with global standards of success, signaling that they've "made it."

---

5. Cultural Fusion: Blending Tradition with Modern Luxury

In India, it's common to see a blend of traditional and modern luxury, where people combine high-end branded items with traditional attire. A bride might wear a traditional silk saree with a Cartier bracelet, or a groom may sport a Rolex with his sherwani. This fusion of East and West showcases a cultural shift—an attempt to balance deep-rooted traditions with contemporary symbols of affluence.

This blend is also seen in the younger generation, who may still value their heritage but are keen to make luxury a part of their modern identity. By wearing branded items alongside traditional symbols, they're creating a new, hybrid expression of success that acknowledges their past while embracing the present. For many, this combination is a way of honoring both family values and personal achievements, a reflection of an evolving cultural identity.

---

6. The Spiritual Side of Luxury: When Material Meets Meaning

In India, luxury isn't just about appearance—it's often tied to spirituality and deeper meaning. Items like gold and silk are seen as auspicious, holding a symbolic value that goes beyond their monetary worth. Many view the act of buying or wearing such items as a way of seeking blessings and honoring family deities. This spiritual aspect of luxury sets it apart from purely materialistic consumerism, as it ties luxury items to a sense of purpose and reverence.

This perspective explains why some people, even those with modest means, are willing to spend on luxury items for religious or cultural events. For them, the purchase is not just a display of wealth, but a way of fulfilling spiritual obligations and expressing gratitude. This approach to luxury offers a unique insight into how culture can transform material items into meaningful symbols.

Key Takeaways

The role of culture and tradition in luxury perception offers a unique perspective on why people seek out branded goods. Here are a few insights to consider:

1. **Luxury as Heritage**: Traditional markers of wealth, such as gold and heirlooms, remain relevant and reflect the deep cultural roots of Indian society. These items symbolize continuity and respect for heritage.
2. **Modern Aspirations, Traditional Foundations**: Western luxury brands have added a layer to the Indian concept of luxury, but they haven't replaced traditional values. Instead, they coexist, creating a unique blend of old and new that reflects India's developing identity.

3. **Social Status and Cultural Norms**: Social gatherings often demand displays of wealth, where luxury items are not just personal choices but reflections of family and societal expectations.

4. **A Fusion of Meanings**: By combining modern branded items with traditional attire, people are crafting a new identity that honors both their heritage and their achievements.

5. **Spiritual Significance of Luxury**: Luxury in India often has a spiritual dimension, where high-value items are seen as more than material possessions—they're symbolic, cultural, and sometimes even sacred.

Final Reflection

Understanding the cultural context of luxury reveals that the desire for branded goods goes beyond mere consumerism; it's tied to family, social norms, and personal values. In India, luxury is as much about honoring tradition as it is about signaling success, creating a unique dynamic that blends the past with the present. This chapter encourages readers to reflect on their own relationship with luxury and consider whether tradition, modern aspirations, or a combination of both influence their choices.

Chapter 14

The Role of Cultural Identity in Branded Goods – A Reflection of Values

Luxury and branded goods are not just about fashion or status; they are deeply intertwined with cultural identity. In India, a country with a rich and diverse cultural heritage, the role of branded goods goes beyond mere consumption — it becomes a reflection of values, traditions, and aspirations. Branded goods can symbolize modernity and global connectivity, but they also serve as markers of individual and collective identity.

For middle-class consumers in India, purchasing branded goods is often influenced by a complex interplay of cultural pride, economic aspirations, and a desire to stay connected to global trends. In this chapter, we will explore how cultural identity shapes the way Indians perceive and engage with branded goods, and how brands, both local and global, leverage cultural elements to appeal to Indian consumers.

The Intersection of Tradition and Modernity in Indian Consumer Culture

India is a country where tradition and modernity often coexist in harmony. While many Indians hold on to their cultural roots, they are also eager to embrace the opportunities and conveniences that come with modernization. This duality is reflected in consumer behavior, particularly in the working class, which is navigating between preserving cultural values and aspiring toward global lifestyles.

For example, a middle-class family may purchase a **luxury saree** for a traditional wedding, a symbol of cultural heritage, while also investing in a **designer handbag** from a global brand for the same occasion. This blending of traditional and modern elements is common in Indian society, where branded goods are used to express both personal style and cultural values.

The challenge for many middle-class consumers is finding a balance between honoring tradition and embracing modernity. Branded goods, especially those from Indian luxury brands, offer a way to do both. Brands like **Fabindia, Ritu Kumar,** and **Sabyasachi** cater to this desire by combining traditional Indian craftsmanship with contemporary design. For many, owning these products is not just about fashion; it's about staying connected to their cultural roots while also presenting themselves as modern and forward-thinking.

The Global Influence: Western Brands and Indian Identity

While Indian brands play a significant role in shaping cultural identity, **global brands** have also made a profound impact on Indian consumers. As more middle-class Indians gain access to global products through e-commerce platforms, Western luxury brands like **Gucci, Louis Vuitton,** and **Apple** have become symbols of global connectivity and success.

For many Indian consumers, purchasing global brands is a way to express their connection to the world beyond their borders. It signals that they are part of a global community, sharing in the same tastes, trends, and experiences as consumers in New York, Paris, or London. This connection to global culture is appealing to the younger middle class, who are more likely to be influenced by Western media, pop culture, and social media influencers.

However, this embrace of Western brands often raises questions about **cultural authenticity**. Some critics argue that the growing influence of Western brands is diluting Indian culture, encouraging consumers to prioritize foreign products over local craftsmanship. Interestingly, many middle-class consumers see their engagement with global brands as a natural part of India's modernization, a reflection of their aspirations to be part of the global economy.

The Re-Emergence of Indian Craftsmanship and Local Brands

In response to the dominance of global brands, there has been a growing movement in India to support **local craftsmanship** and **homegrown luxury brands**. This trend, often referred to as the **"vocal for local"** movement, has gained significant traction, particularly among middle-class consumers who want to celebrate India's rich heritage while also supporting ethical and sustainable practices.

Brands like **Anita Dongre, Good Earth,** and **Jaypore** have successfully positioned themselves as luxury brands that honor Indian traditions. These brands often use traditional Indian textiles, techniques like handloom weaving and block printing, and indigenous materials to create products that are both modern and rooted in cultural heritage.

For middle-class consumers, buying from these brands is not just about owning a beautiful product; it's about participating in a larger cultural narrative. By investing in Indian luxury goods, they are supporting artisans, preserving cultural traditions, and taking pride in their identity. This trend reflects a broader shift in consumer behavior, where branded goods are increasingly seen as expressions of cultural pride rather than just status symbols.

Branded Goods as Cultural Capital

Branded goods serve as **cultural capital** for middle-class consumers in India. Cultural capital refers to the non-financial assets that contribute to one's social mobility, including education, intellect, style, and knowledge of cultural practices. For many middle-class Indians, owning certain branded goods signifies a level of sophistication and cultural awareness.

For example, wearing a **Banarasi saree** from a renowned designer or carrying a **Hermès bag** to a business meeting can convey different forms of cultural capital. The Banarasi saree connects the wearer to India's long tradition of textile craftsmanship, while the Hermès bag signals familiarity with global luxury standards. Both items carry symbolic weight, allowing the owner to navigate different social and cultural contexts.

For the Indian middle class, branded goods often serve as tools for **social negotiation**. They help individuals position themselves within a particular cultural or social group, signaling both their respect for tradition and their embrace of modernity. This dual role of branded goods as both cultural and social capital makes them highly desirable, especially in a country where class distinctions and social mobility are deeply interconnected.

How Brands Leverage Cultural Identity in Marketing

Global and local brands alike are aware of the importance of cultural identity in shaping consumer behavior. Many brands, particularly those operating in India, tailor their marketing strategies to reflect cultural values and traditions, ensuring that their products resonate with Indian consumers.

For example, during festivals like **Diwali** or **Durga Puja**, brands often release special collections or marketing campaigns that celebrate the cultural significance of these events. Luxury brands may create limited-edition products inspired by Indian art or motifs, while global brands may collaborate with Indian designers to create culturally relevant items.

This cultural customization is particularly effective in the Indian market, where festivals and traditional celebrations play a central role in consumer spending. By aligning their products with cultural events, brands create a sense of **relevance** and **emotional connection** with Indian consumers. For the middle class, these culturally tailored products offer a way to participate in both the global luxury market and their own cultural traditions.

The Influence of Bollywood and Celebrity Endorsements

In India, **Bollywood** plays a significant role in shaping cultural identity and consumer preferences. Many luxury and branded goods become popular because they are seen in films or worn by Bollywood celebrities. The influence of Bollywood stars like **Deepika Padukone**, **Shah Rukh Khan**, and **Alia Bhatt** extends beyond the screen, as their endorsement of certain brands can dramatically increase a product's desirability.

For middle-class consumers, buying a product endorsed by a Bollywood celebrity is not just about following a trend — it's about feeling connected to a larger cultural narrative. Bollywood has long reflected Indian society, and its stars are seen as icons of success, beauty, and modernity. By purchasing the brands they endorse, consumers feel as though they are part of the glamorous world of Bollywood, even if only in a small way.

Celebrity endorsements also help brands navigate the complexities of **cultural identity** in India. By associating their products with beloved Bollywood stars, brands can tap into the emotional and cultural significance that these figures hold for Indian consumers. This connection to Bollywood gives branded goods a level of authenticity and relatability that resonates with the middle class.

The Middle-Class Balancing Act: Global Aspirations and Cultural Pride

For the Indian middle class, branded goods often represent a balancing act between **global aspirations** and **cultural pride**. In one aspect, they are drawn to global luxury brands that symbolize success, modernity, and international exposure. Taking pride in supporting Indian craftsmanship and traditions, especially as the country becomes more vocal about its cultural heritage.

This balancing act reflects the broader challenges of navigating a rapidly changing society. As India becomes more integrated into the global economy, middle-class consumers are increasingly exposed to global trends, yet they remain deeply connected to their cultural roots. Branded goods, both local and global, offer a way to express this duality — to show that they can be both modern and traditional, global and local.

For many, the solution lies in **combining elements** from both worlds. A middle-class woman may pair a **Chanel bag** with a traditional Indian outfit, or a businessman might wear a **Rolex watch** while attending a religious festival in traditional attire. These combinations reflect the fluidity of Indian identity, where the lines between tradition and modernity are swinging.

Conclusion: Branded Goods as a Reflection of Indian Identity

In India, branded goods are more than just luxury items or status symbols; they reflect cultural identity. For the economy class, these products allow them to navigate the complexities of modern life, where tradition and modernity often intersect. Whether it's supporting local artisans, embracing global luxury, or finding ways to blend the two, Indian consumers use branded goods to express their values, aspirations, and sense of self.

As the Indian middle class continues to grow and develop, the role of branded goods will probably become even more nuanced. Brands that understand and respect the cultural significance of their products are best positioned to succeed in this dynamic market. For middle-class consumers, the challenge will be to continue finding ways to express their identity through the products they choose, while staying true to both their cultural roots and global ambitions.

Chapter 15

Everyday Luxuries – The Subtle Art of Showing Off

The Travel Showcase

Travel used to be about moving from one place to another. But now, it's an opportunity to showcase luxury at every turn—whether it's a quick trip to the airport, a casual road trip, or even a hike in the mountains. Welcome to **The Travel Showcase**, where every day journeys are now transformed into stages for flaunting branded fashion and accessories, often at the expense of practicality. In this world, a suitcase, a coat, or even a water bottle is not just an item; it's a statement.

---

1. The Airport Fashion Parade

Picture this: you're at the airport, waiting for your flight, and you suddenly realize you're in the middle of what could be a runway show. Passengers, decked out in designer tracksuits and luggage, strut through the terminal like they're about to board a private jet rather than a budget airline. Airports have become a scene straight out of a fashion magazine—an opportunity for travelers to show off their best luxury looks, even if their destination is only a few hours away.

Take Ramesh, for instance. He's flying to Mumbai for a quick two-day work trip, but you wouldn't know it by looking at him. Clad in a crisp Gucci tracksuit, he wheels along a matching Louis Vuitton suitcase so large it looks like he's relocating for a year. The suitcase has more compartments and pockets than he could possibly need, but to Ramesh, it's not just luggage; it's a status symbol.

With oversized Ray-Bans perched on his nose (despite being indoors) and AirPods Max around his neck (though they're not even turned on), Ramesh makes his way through the terminal with the calm confidence of a runway model. He stops occasionally to check his watch—a Rolex, of course—pretending to be oblivious to the envious stares of fellow travelers. In his mind, every step is a moment, every glance a photo op.

Meanwhile, across the terminal, Meera is balancing precariously in Louboutin heels as she sips her carefully crafted latte. She's waiting for her boarding call, but she's turned Gate 24 into her personal photo studio. Her luggage is arranged just so, her Prada tote prominently displayed, and she's perfected the art of the "candid" selfie as if she's just too busy with her glamorous life to notice the camera.

Together, Ramesh and Meera are part of the **Airport Fashion Parade**, where the terminal has become less about transit and more about transformation—a place where travelers can pretend, they're jet-setters living the high life, even if their final destination is just two hours away.

---

2. The Airport Arrival Greeting Game

While most people look a little rumpled and tired after a flight, some see the arrivals area as their grand entrance, a chance to showcase their "celebrity" side. These travelers walk out of the terminal not as weary fliers but as if they're stepping onto the red carpet.

Meet Priya, fresh off a domestic flight but looking like she's returning from an international tour. She steps out in a perfectly draped Burberry trench coat, Gucci handbag slung casually over her shoulder. Her oversized Chanel sunglasses remain in place, even though it's nearly sunset. As she walks toward her family, she glances around to see if anyone's watching, because for Priya, this is more than just a homecoming—it's a performance.

Her parents greet her excitedly, but Priya focused on making her entrance memorable, flips her hair back, casually adjusts her handbag, and strikes a pose that could rival a Bollywood star's airport look. As other families exchange hugs and laughter, Priya's family is part of a fashion moment. Her mother fusses over her look, while Priya gives her a knowing smile—mission accomplished.

For Priya, the **Airport Arrival Greeting Game** isn't about reuniting with family; it's a chance to showcase the high-end lifestyle she's cultivated. Whether anyone actually cares is beside the point. The real achievement is that she walked out looking like a million bucks, regardless of the fact that she's just come off a budget airline.

---

3. Designer Luggage for a Road Trip

In the past, road trips were simple affairs—throw a few bags in the trunk and hit the road. But for some, a road trip is no excuse to skimp on style. Even the most casual weekend getaway becomes an opportunity to showcase luxury travel gear.

Take Arjun, for example. He's heading out with friends for a weekend at a rustic hill station. Most people might toss their belongings into a backpack or duffel bag, but Arjun prefers his Louis Vuitton suitcase, complete with custom initials and a matching Hermès overnight bag. His luggage practically screams "luxury getaway," even though they're staying in a budget guest house where the suitcase will probably sit unnoticed in the corner.

As they load the car, Arjun gives careful instructions on how his luggage should be placed to avoid scuffs or scratches. When his friends suggest a quick tea stop at a roadside stall, Arjun hesitates, visibly anxious about exposing his bags to dust and dirt. "Can we find a nicer spot?" he asks, casting a nervous glance at his pristine luggage.

For Arjun, the experience is all about looking the part. Even if they're roughing it at a guest house, his Louis Vuitton bag gives him the satisfaction of knowing he's elevating the experience—even if no one else seems to notice.

---

4. Branded Water Bottles on a Hike

In the pursuit of nature, many seek simplicity and peace. But for some, hiking is just another backdrop for displaying eco-luxury. Imagine Neha, setting off on a hike with friends, dressed in top-tier Patagonia gear and carrying a sleek, limited-edition S'well bottle. Her gear is less about function and more about the image—a curated selection that signals "luxury nature lover."

As they begin the hike, Neha clutches her water bottle delicately, as though it's made of glass. Her friends are carrying practical plastic bottles, but Neha's bottle is no ordinary accessory. It's an eco-friendly statement piece, meant to keep her water cool for hours and, just as importantly, to look perfect in every photo. She takes careful sips, ensuring the logo is always visible to anyone nearby.

Neha also has her fair share of commentary: "This bottle is designed to preserve minerals, you know," she explains. Her friends exchange bemused glances, but Neha is unfazed. For her, hiking isn't about the views or the exercise—it's about being seen as someone who knows how to do nature in style.

The Branded Water Bottles on a Hike routine turns an otherwise rustic activity into an eco-luxury showcase, where even the simple act of drinking water becomes a branded moment.

In the world of The Travel Showcase, journeys become performances, and every item—whether it's a tracksuit, luggage, or a water bottle—has a role to play in crafting an image. From airports to road trips to hiking trails, the modern traveler is less concerned with the destination than with how they look getting there. In these settings, luxury items serve as props in a carefully staged production, where practicality is cast aside for the sake of appearances.

For the rest of us, these travelers provide a free show—a parade of designer items and branded accessories that turn ordinary journeys into extraordinary displays of status and style. While it's easy to chuckle at the extravagance, there's also a sense of relatability. After all, who doesn't want to look good, even if the journey is a quick flight or a weekend getaway?

In the end, **The Travel Showcase** reminds us that sometimes, the thrill isn't in reaching the destination, but in looking incredible every step of the way.

The Fitness and Wellness Display

Fitness today has moved beyond simply breaking a sweat. In modern gyms, home workouts, and locker rooms, luxury has made its mark. From branded activewear to designer skincare routines, fitness has become a display of wealth, taste, and carefully curated aesthetics. Welcome to **The Fitness and Wellness Display**, where the goal isn't just fitness—it's looking the part, no matter the effort involved.

---

1. Gym Glam – The Branded Workout

Meet Amit, who treats the gym as if it's a high-fashion photoshoot. Dressed in matching Nike Pro leggings, shirt, and shoes, Amit makes sure every logo is visible, down to his custom Beats headphones and Lululemon water bottle. With his Apple Watch tracking his every move, he's more focused on his look than his workout. In between exercises, he checks his reflection in the mirror, adjusting his shirt and smoothing his hair to maintaining his "athletic-chic" image. His workouts are quick, his breaks frequent—perfect for ensuring he's sweat-free but still looks like he's "grinding."

Amit's outfit and accessories are carefully chosen to show off his "serious" approach to fitness, but the truth is, he's more concerned about his gym look than his performance. He's here to make an impression, to look like he's training for a triathlon—even if his actual workout involves a leisurely pace on the elliptical.

---

2. The Gym Locker Room Vanity Parade

Once the workout ends, the real display begins in the locker room. Shruti, for instance, brings along a luxury skincare kit that rivals a department store beauty counter. She sets up her products—a full line of La Mer, Evian facial mist, and even a small jade roller—on the counter. The entire lineup is curated and perfectly arranged.

As Shruti goes through her skincare ritual, she offers advice to anyone watching. "You need to treat your skin well after all that sweating," she says, dabbing on eye cream with the precision of a surgeon. Her routine includes multiple steps, each product applied with care, and by the end, she looks fresh enough to hit the town rather than go home. For Shruti, **The Gym Locker Room Vanity Parade** is about more than skincare; it's a way to flaunt her luxury lifestyle. After all, nothing says "I'm committed to wellness" quite like a 20-minute, post-gym skincare ritual.

3. The High-End Home Workout Setup

For those who prefer to exercise in private, the home gym has become a luxury statement on its own. Meet Veena, whose living room doubles as a high-end workout studio. She's invested in a Peloton bike, a set of designer dumbbells, and a mirror that doubles as a digital trainer. Her yoga mat is a designer piece with monogrammed initials, and her Lululemon resistance bands are color-coordinated with her workout outfits.

The irony? Veena rarely uses her setup. Instead, she spends most of her time organizing and rearranging her gear, making sure everything is perfectly positioned. She'll snap a few photos with captions like "Today's workout goals 💪" for social media, but the actual workout is a quick set of stretches. For Veena, the **High-End Home Workout Setup** is more about having the gear than using it. Her equipment isn't there to be functional; it's there to complete the aesthetic of her home as a luxury wellness haven.

4. Designer Water Bottles on Display

In gyms and on hikes, even water bottles have joined the luxury showcase. Neha arrives at the gym with a sleek, eco-friendly S'well bottle, its metallic finish shining like a piece of jewelry. She carefully sips from it, wiping it down after each drink to keep it fingerprint-free. Unlike her fellow gym-goers, who carry practical plastic bottles, Neha's bottle is less about hydration and more about status.

Throughout her workout, she holds the bottle like a prized accessory, pausing every so often to angle it just right for her mirror selfies. If anyone asks, she explains, "This bottle keeps water cold for hours and is designed for eco-conscious people." Neha's commitment to her bottle is clear: in her world, hydration isn't just functional; it's fashion.

5. The Limited-Edition Sneaker Enthusiast

Beside the treadmill, Priya stands with her exclusive Nike trainers, part of a limited edition that cost her a small fortune. These aren't just gym shoes; they're collector's items, and Priya takes pride in explaining the exclusivity of her sneakers to anyone who asks. Her workout is mostly a series of light stretches, nothing that might risk scuffing her prized footwear.

Every so often, Priya glances down at her shoes, inspecting them for any sign of wear. After all, the point of her gym visit isn't to push herself physically—it's to display the shoes. She's perfected the art of looking active without actually engaging in anything strenuous, ensuring her shoes remain pristine. For Priya, the gym is just a showroom for her sneakers, a place to enjoy her "exclusive drop" without putting it to the test.

6. The Social Media Athlete

Then there's Rahul, a self-proclaimed fitness influencer whose workouts are more about content creation than calorie burn. Dressed in an Under Armour shirt, limited-edition Adidas sneakers, and a smartwatch, Rahul arrives with a portable ring light and tripod. His focus is less on his workout and more on getting the perfect shot for his followers.

Rahul's "workout" consists of a few reps, followed by strategic pauses to check his reflection and adjust his posture. Every ten minutes, he takes a break to snap selfies, making sure the brand logos are prominently displayed. He ends the session with a motivational caption like "Putting in the work 💪 #FitnessLife #LuxuryWellness." His followers don't know that his workout was more about posing than pushing limits. For Rahul, the gym is a stage where every rep is a chance to impress.

---

7. The Designer Yoga Mat Display

In the yoga room, Meera has set up her space with the precision of an art installation. She rolls out her designer Manduka yoga mat, complete with embroidered edges and her initials subtly stitched in one corner. Her matching yoga towel is carefully spread over the mat, each fold perfectly aligned. Meera's attire is coordinated as well—an Alo Yoga set in pastel tones that matches her mat.

As she moves through her poses, she ensures her hair and outfit remain in place, adjusting between stretches to maintain her "effortlessly chic" look. After the session, she takes a few photos of her setup, captioning one of them "Zen vibes only #YogaLife #LuxuryFitness." For Meera, the gym is more than a place to exercise; it's a curated experience, where even yoga becomes an opportunity to showcase style.

In **The Fitness and Wellness Display**, the gym and home workout spaces become backdrops for a curated lifestyle. For people like Amit,

Shruti, Veena, Neha, Priya, and Rahul, fitness is less about health and more about the image they project. From branded activewear to designer water bottles and skincare, every item serves a purpose beyond functionality. It's ironic that, these luxury enthusiasts treat the gym like a fashion show, the locker room as a beauty salon, and home workout gear as decor rather than equipment.

Social Moments as Showcases

Social gatherings—dinner parties, weddings, even coffee shop meet-ups—were once simple opportunities to connect. But today, these events have taken on a new role: they're prime stages for showing off branded accessories, designer outfits, and the latest luxury purchases. Welcome to **Social Moments as Showcases**, where every social event transforms into a display of luxury, style, and status.

---

1. Coffee Shop Couture

The humble coffee shop has become a catwalk for luxury, where every order of a latte or espresso is accompanied by a meticulously curated setup of designer accessories. Meet Ria, who's meeting her friends at a café. But for her, this isn't just a casual coffee—it's an opportunity to showcase her latest acquisitions.

Dressed in a Prada trench coat and carrying a mini-Hermès purse, Ria arranges her belongings on the table with precision. Her iPhone is encased in a leather Gucci case, and next to her cappuccino, she places a Montblanc pen (though she has no intention of writing anything). She even adjusts her coffee cup for a perfect "candid" photo to post later with a caption like, "Coffee vibes with the essentials ☕🧋."

Throughout the meet-up, Ria barely touches her coffee. Instead, she's focused on adjusting her look and casually name-dropping her recent shopping spree in Dubai. Her friends roll their eyes but smile politely. For Ria, **Coffee Shop Couture** is less about caffeine and more about creating an image—because in the age of social media, a simple coffee outing is a chance to flaunt her luxury lifestyle.

2. The Dinner Party Display

Dinner parties have evolved from intimate gatherings to sophisticated exhibitions of luxury tableware, decor, and designer outfits. Take Sameer, who loves to host "casual" dinners at his upscale apartment. But Sameer's version of casual involves imported dinnerware, custom-embroidered napkins, and candle holders from an exclusive home decor line.

As guests arrive, they're greeted with champagne in crystal flutes and a table that looks like it belongs in a five-star restaurant. Sameer explains the origins of each item, detailing how his plates were hand-painted by artisans in Italy and how the silverware was a gift from a "very dear friend" in Paris. When one guest asked where the food was, Sameer reassured them, "It's all about the experience here, not just the meal."

Throughout the evening, Sameer casually steers conversations toward his recent travels and investments, all the while keeping an eye on his guests to make sure they're suitably impressed. For Sameer, the **Dinner Party Display** isn't about food or friendship—it's an opportunity to subtly remind everyone of his taste and status.

3. The Wedding Bling Battle

Indian weddings have always been vibrant, but now they've become a battleground for luxury fashion. Guests compete to outshine each other, and sometimes, even the bride and groom become secondary to the spectacle. Take Meera, attending her cousin's wedding in an elaborate Sabyasachi saree, diamond jewelry that could rival a royal, and enough bangles to fill a jewelry store.

Throughout the ceremony, Meera makes sure her outfit catches every light, striking subtle poses and ensuring every piece of jewelry is visible. When family members compliment her, she waves them off with a laugh, saying, "Oh, this is just something simple I put together." Her friends, meanwhile, are busy calculating the combined value of her attire.

As the evening progresses, other guests join the **Wedding Bling Battle**, each trying to display the most luxurious jewelry and attire. The bride may be the star, but Meera ensures she isn't outshined. In her mind, weddings aren't just about celebrating love—they're a stage to flaunt wealth and taste in a grand, public way.

---

4. The Branded Picnic

A simple picnic has been transformed into an upscale display, where the setting is as curated as the food. Rashmi invites her friends for an "outdoor escape" in the park, complete with designer picnic baskets, Ralph Lauren blankets, and artisanal snacks sourced from specialty stores.

Each dish is perfectly arranged on porcelain plates, and Rashmi carefully photographs the setup before anyone is allowed to touch the food. Her picnic basket is filled with cheeses that come with their own backstories, and she offers a guided tasting of her favorite wines. Her friends are charmed, though slightly puzzled by the level of detail and planning. Rashmi explains, "It's all about bringing luxury to every experience."

By the end of the picnic, most of the food is barely touched, but the photos are perfect. For Rashmi, the **Branded Picnic** is less about eating and more about capturing a picturesque moment. She leaves the park satisfied, knowing her followers will see her as the ultimate hostess, who brings elegance wherever she goes.

---

5. Designer Water Bottles on Display

At social gatherings, even water bottles have become part of the luxury showcase. Neha, for instance, never leaves home without her eco-friendly S'well bottle in hand. At any event, she places it on the table like a prized accessory. When a friend offers her a glass of water, she declines, saying, "I only drink from this—it keeps the minerals intact."

The bottle itself is metallic, sleek, and expensive-looking, almost like a piece of jewelry. Neha cradles it like a trophy, making sure to highlight how it's designed for both functionality and elegance. In a world of plastic bottles, her designer option stands out, a silent nod to her "elite" approach to hydration.

---

6. The Fine Dining Experience at Home

For some, hosting a dinner party isn't just about food—it's a showcase for gourmet cooking skills and exclusive ingredients. Take Arjun, who invites friends over for what he calls a "simple dinner," but there's nothing simple about it. He lines the kitchen counter with truffle oil, pink Himalayan salt, and imported cheeses, each item deliberately chosen to impress.

As Arjun plates each dish, he describes the origins of each ingredient with a level of detail that rivals a chef's tasting menu. "This balsamic vinegar is from a small farm in Modena," he says, watching as his guests politely nod. For Arjun, the **Fine Dining Experience at Home** isn't about serving a meal; it's about creating an ambiance that speaks to his "refined" taste.

---

7. The Gift-Giving Gala

Gift exchanges are a new way to showcase one's status, even at casual celebrations. Picture Priya at her friend's baby shower. Instead of bringing a simple baby outfit or a toy, Priya's gift is a luxury baby blanket from a high-end children's boutique, wrapped in custom, embossed paper.

As everyone else hands over their thoughtful (and budget-friendly) gifts, Priya's present steals the spotlight, drawing admiring glances from other guests. She casually explains, "I wanted something memorable and unique." The friend is grateful, but visibly overwhelmed. For Priya, the **Gift-Giving Gala** isn't about the recipient—it's a chance to showcase her taste for exclusive items that stand out.

8. The Branded Family Photoshoot

In the age of social media, even family photoshoots have become luxurious displays. Rajesh has organized a family shoot for the festive season, but it's less about the photos and more about the outfits. All of his family members dressed in coordinated Burberry sweaters, with his young daughter in a tiny Gucci dress.

As the photographer captures candid shots, Rajesh ensures every brand logo is clearly visible, occasionally stopping to adjust his son's pose to make sure the designer label on his jacket is front and center. For Rajesh, the **Branded Family Photoshoot** is about more than capturing memories; it's a visual display of his family's luxury lifestyle.

In **Social Moments as Showcases**, every gathering—no matter how casual—becomes a chance to flaunt luxury and sophistication. For people like Ria, Sameer, Meera, Rashmi, and Neha, social events aren't just about connecting; they're opportunities to display their high-end lifestyles. Whether it's a coffee meet up, a dinner party, a wedding, or a simple picnic, these gatherings are meticulously curated to project taste, wealth, and status.

For these socialites, every glass, napkin, and accessory tell a story. They don't just attend events; they turn each moment into a stage, ensuring that their luxury choices are noticed and admired. While others focus on friendships or festivities, they're focused on impressions. In their world, social gatherings are more than moments to connect—they're showcases for their carefully crafted, brand-conscious lives.

Luxury in Everyday Errands

Errands—grocery shopping, running to the office, or a quick stop at the store—were once mundane tasks. But today, these everyday activities have turned into stages for showing off high-end taste, where designer bags, luxury accessories, and even eco-conscious choices all send a message. Welcome to **Luxury in Everyday Errands**, where even the simplest task is an opportunity to demonstrate a little extra glamour.

---

1. Designer Grocery Runs

Gone are the days of quick, practical grocery shopping. Now, grocery stores have become unofficial runways, with shoppers dressing up and carrying branded bags as if they're at a premiere. Take Priya, for example, who never steps into her neighborhood supermarket without her designer tote and a carefully curated outfit.

Priya's grocery tote is a sleek Gucci canvas bag, designed more for fashion than function, and she's dressed in a Ralph Lauren blazer with a pair of understated, but clearly expensive, loafers. As she glides down the produce aisle, she pauses to check her reflection in the glass doors of the refrigerated section, adjusting her hair and posing briefly with a basket of organic avocados. Each item she picks seems hand-selected to look just right in her cart.

For Priya, the grocery store isn't just about buying essentials—it's about creating an experience, a moment that says, "I'm living my best life." Her quick grocery run is really an opportunity to showcase her high-end taste, making **Designer Grocery Runs** more about appearances than produce.

2. Work Desk Decorations

In today's workspaces, the humble desk has become a canvas for self-expression and, often, a display of luxury. Meet Sameer, an office professional who has turned his desk into a mini luxury showroom. His workspace, adorned with high-end gadgets and accessories: a Montblanc pen on a leather-bound notebook, a custom brass paperweight, and a Hermès coffee mug that sits like a trophy beside his computer.

Sameer's desk setup is meticulously organized, each item placed for maximum visibility. His MacBook rests on a handcrafted leather stand, and now and then, he casually mentions how much he values "quality materials" and "workplace aesthetics." His coworkers chuckle, but Sameer is serious—his desk is his sanctuary, a place where his personal taste can shine through.

For Sameer, **Work Desk Decorations** aren't just about organization—they're about cultivating an aura of sophistication. He's less concerned with deadlines and more invested in ensuring his desk reflects his upscale lifestyle. After all, the true mark of success is a desk that says, "I've arrived."

3. Fine Dining at Home

A simple meal at home can become an elaborate affair when you have a taste for high-end decor and luxury ingredients. Arjun invites a few friends over for dinner, calling it a "casual gathering." But when they arrive, they're greeted by a table set with silverware, hand-painted plates from Italy, and cloth napkins embroidered with his initials.

Arjun describes each ingredient in his dishes with the finesse of a Michelin-starred chef. "This truffle oil is imported from a small town in Italy," he explains, pouring it carefully over a plate of pasta. "And the sea salt? That's Himalayan pink salt, hand-harvested." As his friends dig in, he offers tasting notes on each wine, pausing in between, letting them to appreciate the complexity.

For Arjun, **Fine Dining at Home** isn't just about feeding his guests—it's about creating an experience that feels exclusive, sophisticated, and, of course, memorable. His friends are charmed, though slightly bemused by the level of detail, but Arjun knows he's made his point: even a simple dinner can become a luxury event with the right touch.

---

4. The Kids' Birthday Extravaganza

For some parents, even children's birthday parties become opportunities to showcase luxury taste and style. Ritu, for example, has organized her son's birthday as a designer-themed event. The decor includes color-coordinated balloons, custom cake toppers with gold accents, and personalized gift bags for each little guest.

Ritu's son, dressed in a Ralph Lauren mini suit, looks more like a model than a toddler. When other parents ask about the decor, she explains, "I just want the best for him." The party is filled with carefully curated snacks, boutique decorations, and a miniature photo booth for parents to capture the experience.

For Ritu, the **Kids' Birthday Extravaganza** is a chance to showcase her taste and creativity, transforming her child's celebration into a luxury event. As other parents watch, Ritu feels satisfied knowing she's hosted a party that's as stylish as it is memorable.

---

6. The Ultimate Car Wash Experience

For some, even a trip to the car wash becomes an opportunity to flaunt luxury. Take Vikram, who insists on only the best for his luxury SUV. He arrives at the premium car wash, requesting the "VIP treatment" package, which includes hand-waxing, custom detailing, and interior scent selection.

As his car undergoes the spa-like treatment, Vikram makes sure to supervise, occasionally reminding the staff, "Please be careful with the leather." After the car is spotless, he takes a few photos to share with his friends, tagging the service as "Only the best for my ride." For Vikram, **The Ultimate Car Wash Experience** is more than maintenance; it's an event worthy of admiration.

---

7. The Fancy Gym Bag for a Quick Errand

For some, a quick stop at the bank or a pharmacy calls for high-fashion accessories. Mira, heading out to run errands, carries a designer gym bag—not because she's going to the gym, but because it's "too beautiful" to leave at home.

Her workout bag is a Chanel duffel, and even though she's just buying shampoo, she makes sure it's prominently displayed. Mira treats every store aisle as a runway, casually adjusting the bag on her shoulder and looking around to see if anyone notices her designer accessory. For Mira, **The Fancy Gym Bag** for a Quick Errand isn't just practical—it's a statement.

---

8. The Luxury Errand Shoes

For some, running errands requires the right footwear. Sanjay insists on wearing his Tod's loafers even for a quick trip to the convenience store. He moves slowly, mindful of every step, avoiding any risk of scuffing his prized shoes.

In the store, Sanjay doesn't just grab his items; he saunters through the aisles, adjusting his posture as if he's in a showroom rather than a grocery store. For him, **The Luxury Errand Shoes** aren't just for comfort—they're a way to show that even the smallest task is worth doing in style.

Luxury in Everyday Errands, even the simplest outings become opportunities for showcasing taste and status. From car washes and quick stops to designer bags and premium footwear, people like Vikram, Mira, and Sanjay demonstrate that there's no errand too small for a touch of glamor. While others rush through their day, these luxury enthusiasts take their time, savoring each moment as a chance to flaunt their lifestyle.

For them, each item—whether it's a bag, a pair of shoes, or a car—is not just an accessory but a part of their identity. By transforming everyday tasks into moments of elegance, they remind us that sometimes, life's simplest moments can be the most fashionable.

Pet Pampering and Parenting Display

For some, it's not enough to flaunt their own designer items—they extend the luxury to their pets and children, turning park visits and walks into showcases of high-end taste. Welcome to **Pet Pampering and Parenting Display**, where dogs wear couture collars, babies ride in designer strollers, and everything is a statement of style.

---

1. Branded Baby Strollers in the Park

Parents strolling through the park with their children used to be a humble, everyday affair. But now, even baby gear has become a status symbol, and parents turn their little ones' strollers into rolling luxury displays. Take Ananya, for instance, who arrives at the park with her toddler in a Bugaboo stroller—complete with a monogrammed cover and gold-accented wheels.

Ananya has dressed her baby in a tiny Ralph Lauren onesie, a matching sun hat, and miniature shoes that cost more than a grown adult's. As they enter the park, other parents glance admiringly at her setup, some even murmuring compliments for her "sense of style." Ananya soaks it in, proudly adjusting her stroller to ensure the logo is visible, and checking that her child's hat is perfectly positioned for photos.

When a fellow parent casually asks where she found such a chic stroller, Ananya smiles modestly. "Oh, it's a custom design. I wanted something that reflects his personality," she says. For her, **Branded Baby Strollers in the Park** is more than a walk; it's a mini fashion show, and her child is the star.

---

2. The Branded Dog Walker

Even pets have become part of the luxury showcase, with every walk transforming into a high-end display of collars, leashes, and pet accessories. Rohan, who takes his French Bulldog, Coco, for walks in a Burberry leash and matching collar set. Coco is dressed in a tiny Gucci sweater, carefully chosen to coordinate with Rohan's own outfit—a casual, but designer, jacket and jeans combo.

As they stroll through the neighborhood, Rohan pauses often, making sure Coco's collar is visible and that the sweater doesn't have a single wrinkle. When other dog owners comment on Coco's outfit, Rohan gives a humble nod, as if it's just another day in the life of a "fashion-forward" pet. "Coco has standards," he says with a grin, explaining how his dog "prefers" high-quality fabrics.

The walk becomes a mini social event, with other pet owners admiring Coco's look and asking for style tips. For Rohan, **The Branded Dog Walker** is less about Coco's exercise and more about displaying his pet's "refined" lifestyle. Coco, blissfully unaware of the spectacle, enjoys the attention while Rohan basks in the compliments.

---

3. Matching Outfits for Kids and Pets

Taking things a step further, some parents and pet owners embrace matching outfits, creating a visual statement that ties together family members—both human and canine. Kavita, for example, has coordinated her weekend outfit with her daughter and her dog, Pepper. Each family member sports a look from the same designer, with Kavita in a floral-print sundress, her daughter in a miniature version, and Pepper in a custom floral-print bandana.

As they walk through the park, passersby can't help but smile at the coordinated look, and Kavita beams as she catches admiring glances. She pauses for a quick photoshoot, positioning her daughter and dog side by side and adjusting everyone's outfits to make sure the labels are clearly visible. When someone asks about the matching look, Kavita replies, "We believe in family style—it's a way of bonding."

For Kavita, **Matching Outfits for Kids and Pets** isn't just cute; it's a chance to create a high-fashion family moment that shows her commitment to aesthetic harmony. The park becomes their runway, and each step is part of a carefully planned scene.

---

4. The Luxury Pet Playdate

Pet playdates have become a social event where pet owners showcase the best of their pets' wardrobes, gear, and accessories. Arjun, a proud dog dad, invites friends for a playdate with his Chihuahua, Simba. But this isn't an ordinary outing; it's a high-end pet gathering, complete with designer dog toys, gourmet treats, and a branded blanket that Arjun spreads out in the center of the park.

Simba arrives in a Moncler dog vest, while Arjun carefully sets out a lineup of luxury chew toys from a boutique pet store. He chats with the other pet owners, explaining how "only the best" will do for Simba, and offers tips on where to find exclusive pet gear. The playdate is as much for the owners as it is for the pets, with each dog's outfit scrutinized and admired.

As the dogs chase each other around, Arjun maintains Simba's "pristine" look, occasionally smoothing out his vest and snapping photos. For Arjun, the **Luxury Pet Playdate** is about much more than socializing; it's about creating a sophisticated setting where he can flaunt Simba's premium lifestyle.

In **Pet Pampering and Parenting Display**, luxury extends beyond oneself, transforming even pets and children into showcases of style and status. For people like Ananya, Rohan, Kavita, and Arjun, the goal is not just to take a stroll or have a playdate—it's presenting their lifestyle as elegant, coordinated, and tastefully high-end. From branded strollers to luxury dog outfits, every detail is carefully curated to make a statement.

These luxury lovers turn everyday outings into mini fashion shows, where even children and pets play their part in showcasing the family's elevated taste. They embody the idea that status can be reflected through one's closest companions, creating a spectacle that's as entertaining as it is aspirational. After all, in the world of luxury, no family member—whether two-legged or four—should miss out on the opportunity to shine.

The Leisure and Vacation Gallery

In the age of luxury, even leisure and vacation activities have become opportunities to showcase status. The poolside, the beach, and even temples are now stages for designer accessories, premium gadgets, and carefully curated outfits. Welcome to **The Leisure and Vacation Gallery**, where relaxation is secondary to presentation, and every moment of reflection or fun comes with a touch of luxury.

---

1. Poolside Style – The Beach and Pool as Stages

For many, a day by the pool or beach is about relaxation and a bit of fun in the sun. But for others, it's the ultimate opportunity to display luxury, where every accessory is chosen not for practicality, but for style. Take Shreya, who arrives at a high-end resort pool with all the essentials: a wide-brimmed sun hat from Chanel, a silk Hermès scarf tied around her waist, and designer flip-flops that cost more than the average hotel room.

Shreya finds a sun lounger in the center of the pool deck and proceeds to arrange her accessories like props in a photoshoot. She lays out her Dior beach towel, making sure the logo is clearly visible, and places a pair of Versace sunglasses on top, even though she's already wearing another pair. As she lounges, she flips through a magazine (also designer-branded) and casually snaps selfies, angling each shot to capture the pool and her perfectly arranged items.

The irony? Shreya never actually dips a toe in the pool. For her, **Poolside Style – The Beach and Pool as Stages** isn't about swimming or sunbathing—it's about setting up a scene that radiates effortless glamor. As far as she's concerned, the pool itself is merely the background for her luxury display.

---

2. The Hotel Poolside Photoshoot

While some come to the hotel pool for a relaxing swim, others see it as a backdrop for a luxury photoshoot. Meet Karan, a travel influencer who approaches poolside settings like a professional model. Armed with his iPhone, a portable tripod, and a high-end camera, Karan's goal isn't to unwind but to capture the perfect "just chilling" look for social media.

Karan's poolside attire is meticulously planned: a designer swimsuit, a Bulgari watch, and a Rolex that he carefully positions on his wrist. He spends several minutes setting up his tripod, adjusting the angle and lighting to get the best possible shot. Between photos, he consults his friend, who's acting as his "stylist," to ensure every item—from his sandals to his sunglasses—is aligned for maximum visual impact.

After dozens of snaps, Karan reviews the photos, selecting the best one to caption with "Living my best life ☼ #VacationVibes." He finally settles back on his sun lounger, satisfied with the outcome, though he still hasn't touched the water. For Karan, **The Hotel Poolside Photoshoot** is about capturing the perfect image—not for himself, but for his audience, who believe he's living the ultimate luxury life.

---

3. The Designer Outfit for a Temple Visit

Even visits to religious sites have become opportunities to flaunt style. Picture Priya, who's heading to a temple for a family ritual but sees no reason why she can't make it a fashionable occasion. She arrives dressed in a beautiful, hand-embroidered saree, a silk shawl draped over her shoulders, and a subtle but unmistakable designer clutch.

As she walks up the temple steps, Priya moves slowly, making sure her saree flows elegantly and her jewelry catches the light. She pauses for a moment, posing by a decorative pillar, where a family member takes her photo. The temple, for Priya, is as much a sacred place as it is a setting for a traditional-meets-luxury photoshoot.

While others focus on the ritual, Priya is busy adjusting her shawl and jewelry, blending her devotion with a touch of high-end style. For her, **The Designer Outfit for a Temple Visit** is about balancing tradition with a hint of exclusivity. She feels that there's no reason faith and fashion can't coexist, especially if there's an opportunity for a memorable Instagram post.

---

4. The Luxury Tech in the Conference Room

Business meetings may sound serious, but for some, they're the perfect setting to flaunt high-end tech gear. Meet Rajesh, a senior executive who arrives at every conference room armed with the latest gadgets, each one meticulously chosen to make a statement. He walks in with a MacBook Pro in a custom leather case, an iPad Pro with a matching Apple Pencil.

Rajesh sets up his workspace with the precision of an artist, arranging his tech items so that every logo is visible. As the meeting begins, he taps his Apple Watch, syncing it with his other devices while dropping casual remarks like, "The seamless integration is a game-changer." When a coworker asks to borrow his pen, he hands over his Montblanc, subtly mentioning its "incredible smoothness" as he does.

For Rajesh, **The Luxury Tech in the Conference Room** is less about the meeting agenda and more about reinforcing his reputation as someone with refined taste. The devices aren't just tools—they're symbols of his success, and he wants his colleagues to know it.

In **The Leisure and Vacation Gallery**, moments of relaxation, reflection, and even spirituality become stages for luxury displays. For people like Shreya, Karan, Priya, and Rajesh, these settings are less about unwinding and more about curating an image of success, taste, and elegance. Whether it's by the pool, at a temple, or in a business meeting, each setting is transformed into a mini photoshoot, where every accessory, gadget, and outfit contributes to a carefully crafted image.

These luxury lovers turn leisurely settings into meticulously planned scenes, where appearances take precedence over experience. Whether it's a photoshoot by the pool or a designer outfit for a sacred space, they believe that every moment should look as glamorous as it feels. After all, in the world of luxury, even relaxation demands style.

The Social Media Chronicles

In today's world, social media is the ultimate stage for luxury displays. People present everything from high-end cars to branded outfits, aiming to impress followers and create the perfect image. Welcome to **The Social Media Chronicles**, where every post is a chance to flaunt a brand, amplify success, and ensure that life looks as glamorous as possible—whether or not it actually is.

---

1. Car Selfies and Branded Drives

For some, a luxury car isn't just a vehicle; it's a prop for the perfect social media post. Meet Akash, who recently upgraded to a sleek Mercedes-Benz and is determined to show his followers every angle. His social media feed has transformed into a gallery of car selfies, each photo more carefully staged than the last.

Akash has mastered the art of the "casual" car photo. He poses behind the wheel with one hand on the gearshift, gazing off into the distance as if deep in thought. He strategically positions his designer watch on his wrist, catching the light, while he makes sure the Mercedes logo is prominently featured in every shot. Akash captions each post with hashtags like #DriveLuxury and #MercedesLife, as if he's giving his followers a glimpse into his effortlessly lavish lifestyle.

But Akash's "branded drives" don't stop there. He's been known to park his car in scenic locations—city skylines, beachfronts, mountain views—just for a quick photo op. Sometimes, he even drives to the outskirts of town to find the perfect sunset for his car's background.

For Akash, **Car Selfies and Branded Drives** aren't about the journey; they're about turning every drive into a luxury moment that his followers will envy.

2. Designer Coffee Shots and Branded Accessories

People often fill social media feeds with perfectly curated coffee shots, but for some, these posts aren't just about caffeine—they're a luxury statement. Neha, for instance, has made an art out of posting photos of her morning lattes, each one accompanied by a carefully arranged set of branded accessories.

She meticulously sets her table: a Hermès scarf draped beside her coffee cup, a Prada purse casually in the background, and her iPhone with its designer case placed just so. She often writes captions like, "Starting my day right," followed by a series of luxury-themed hashtags: #CoffeeAndChic #HermèsLife #PradaLover. Her followers see a glimpse of her "typical" morning, but Neha knows it's anything but typical—it's a staged showcase of her luxury lifestyle.

For Neha, **Designer Coffee Shots and Branded Accessories** are a way to show her followers that she lives elegantly, even in small moments. The coffee isn't the focus; it's the luxurious setup that matters, transforming an ordinary beverage into a high-fashion scene.

3. The Airport "Jetsetter" Look

Few social media moments are as carefully staged as the airport check-in photo, and Karan has perfected this "jetsetter" aesthetic. Every time he flies, Karan posts a photo in front of the departure gate, suitcase beside him, wearing a coordinated travel outfit that screams designer.

Karan's go to set up includes a Louis Vuitton carry-on, a Burberry scarf draped casually over his shoulders, and sunglasses perched just so. He captions his posts with wanderlust-inspired hashtags like #NextStopParis or #JetsetLife, even if he's only going for a weekend getaway. His followers admire his "glamorous" travel routine, but Karan knows it's all carefully curated.

In reality, Karan spends more time planning his airport look and taking photos than he does actually enjoying his destination. For him, **The Airport "Jetsetter" Look** is about crafting an image of effortless style and sophistication, projecting an idealized version of his life where every flight is a fashion moment.

---

4. "Casual" Luxury Outfit Posts

For some, even the simplest outfit is an opportunity for a high-end photoshoot. Take Priya, who refers to her fashion posts as her "casual looks" but spends hours coordinating each piece. She fills her social media feed with images of herself lounging in "relaxed" poses, wearing what she calls "everyday wear"—think Chanel ballet flats, a Gucci belt, and a classic Burberry trench.

Priya's captions are lighthearted— "Just a casual day out" or "Keeping it simple"—but her outfit and backdrop are anything but simple. She poses on cobblestone streets, upscale cafes, and boutiques, ensuring each background complements her attire. Every post is meticulously planned, from the lighting to the composition, capturing the essence of an "unbothered" luxury lifestyle.

For Priya, **"Casual" Luxury Outfit Posts** aren't about authenticity; they're about creating a visual story that suggests her life is effortlessly glamorous. Her followers may not realize the effort that goes into each "casual" photo, but for Priya, that's the point—to make luxury look like a natural part of her day-to-day life.

---

5. The Luxury Gym Selfie

In today's social media world, even fitness is a luxury performance. Rahul, a fitness enthusiast with a penchant for high-end gear, has made his Instagram a gallery of gym selfies featuring designer workout clothes and branded water bottles. He arrives at the gym with a Lululemon shirt, Under Armour shorts, and a custom S'well water bottle that he keeps within reach, always ready for a quick snapshot.

Rahul's workout routine includes plenty of breaks, each one timed for the perfect selfie. He adjusts his posture, makes sure his muscles are flexed, and takes a quick photo, handpicking the best angle to show off both his physique and his gear. He captions these posts with motivational quotes like "Strive for progress, not perfection" and hashtags like #LuxuryFitness and #LululemonLife.

For Rahul, **The Luxury Gym Selfie** is as essential as the workout itself. The gym isn't just a place to stay fit; it's a backdrop for his luxury lifestyle, where every piece of gear is as important as the reps he completes.

In **The Social Media Chronicles**, every moment—whether it's a drive, a coffee, or a workout—becomes a carefully crafted post meant to showcase luxury and sophistication. For people like Akash, Neha, Karan, Priya, and Rahul, social media isn't just a platform; it's a gallery where every post adds to their image of a polished, enviable lifestyle. Each scene is staged to suggest that luxury is part of their everyday routine, even if the reality is far less glamorous.

These social media enthusiasts turn everyday moments into opportunities for high-end performance, curating life to look as pristine and elegant as possible. In a world where every "casual" shot takes hours to perfect, they show that social media is as much about presentation as it is about connection. For them, life isn't just lived—it's styled, staged, and shared, with every detail carefully designed to leave a lasting impression.

As we look back on these scenes of everyday luxury, it's hard not to smile at the irony—and perhaps even see a bit of ourselves in the mix. From the poolside photo shoots and branded baby strollers to designer gym selfies and curated coffee shots, each moment reveals an unspoken truth about modern life: the subtle art of showing off has become woven into our daily routines, often without us even realizing it.

These displays offer a fascinating glimpse into the lengths we go for validation and status. With each brand label, luxury accessory, and carefully staged photo, there's a deeper message: the quest to be seen, admired, and perhaps envied. And while these every day "catwalks" can be entertaining to witness (or participate in), they also remind us of the relentless pursuit of perfection that comes with projecting a certain image.

But beyond the designer logos, filtered photos, and high-end accessories, what is it we're truly looking for? The reality is that many of these moments are fleeting, their satisfaction as temporary as the Instagram likes they gather. Real fulfillment often lies outside the realm of luxury goods. It's found in experiences that don't require a brand label, in relationships that don't need an expensive backdrop, and in a sense of contentment that comes from authenticity rather than appearances.

While there's no harm in enjoying nice things or embracing the occasional indulgence, this journey through the world of everyday luxuries serves as a gentle reminder. The things that truly enrich our lives are rarely the ones that come with a designer price tag. As we strive for a balance between appreciating quality and letting go of the need to impress, we can begin to see that happiness isn't measured by what we show, but by how genuinely we live.

So, let's laugh at the quirks, enjoy the humor, and embrace the freedom that comes from knowing we don't need a luxury brand to feel valuable. Because life's most beautiful moments don't need an audience—they just need us to be present.

Chapter 16

Luxury and Mental Health – The Hidden Costs of Comparison Culture

In an age of social media and digital connectivity, luxury is no longer confined to private spaces; it's publicly displayed and constantly shared. Platforms like Instagram, Facebook, and TikTok have created a culture of constant comparison where we're regularly exposed to snapshots of others' curated lifestyles. While luxury goods may bring temporary satisfaction, the pressure to keep up can have lasting effects on mental health, leading to stress, anxiety, and dissatisfaction. In this chapter, we'll delve into the psychological toll of comparison culture and explore ways to cultivate a healthier relationship with luxury.

---

1. The Comparison Trap – How Social Media Drives Dissatisfaction

Social media can make luxury seem ubiquitous, showing us endless images of people enjoying branded items, luxury vacations, and high-end experiences. Seeing others live "luxuriously" can trigger feelings of inadequacy, leading us to question our choices and circumstances. This phenomenon, known as the "comparison trap," often results in an unrealistic perception of other people's lives.

Studies have shown that excessive social media use is linked to lower self-esteem and higher levels of anxiety, particularly when people compare themselves to others' seemingly perfect lives. Psychologists suggest that comparing ourselves to others is a natural human tendency, but social media amplifies it by providing a never-ending stream of curated images. As a result, many find themselves feeling inadequate, even if they're financially stable and content in other areas of life.

The constant exposure to luxury lifestyles can create a cycle of envy and desire, leaving people feeling like they need to buy more to "keep up" with their peers. This trap leads not only to financial strain but also to an unending pursuit of material validation, which rarely brings lasting happiness.

---

2. The Temporary Satisfaction of Luxury – The "Hedonic Treadmill"

While buying luxury items can provide a temporary boost in happiness, research shows that this satisfaction doesn't last. Psychologists refer to this phenomenon as the "hedonic treadmill," where people quickly adapt to new possessions, returning to their baseline level of happiness shortly after the initial excitement fades. This adaptation process can create a cycle of consumption, where people continually seek new purchases to maintain their sense of happiness.

The hedonic treadmill can lead to a pattern of constantly upgrading or replacing items to recapture the fleeting pleasure of a new purchase. Over time, this cycle can cause feelings of emptiness or dissatisfaction, as the anticipated happiness from luxury items rarely endures. The mental toll of this cycle becomes more pronounced when combined with social pressure, as people feel compelled to keep buying in order to meet societal expectations.

Breaking free from the hedonic treadmill requires a shift in focus from external validation to internal contentment. This involves learning to appreciate non-material aspects of life and cultivating a sense of gratitude for what we already have.

---

3. Financial Stress and Mental Health

The financial burden of keeping up with luxury culture can be significant, especially for those on an economical budget. Many people stretch themselves thin financially to afford high-end items, leading to credit card debt, reduced savings, and financial insecurity. This strain can take a serious toll on mental health, causing anxiety, stress, and even depression.

In addition, financial stress can affect relationships, work performance, and overall well-being. Constantly worrying about money reduces one's ability to enjoy life fully, and the stress of living beyond one's means often outweighs the temporary happiness of owning branded items. For those who find themselves in a cycle of spending for social validation, it's essential to recognize the impact of financial stress on mental health and consider healthier alternatives for self-expression and happiness.

4. The Influence of Advertising and the Power of FOMO

Advertising plays a powerful role in shaping our desires, often creating a sense of "FOMO" (fear of missing out) that drives luxury consumption. Advertisers use persuasive language, celebrity endorsements, and emotionally charged imagery to portray that luxury is essential for happiness, status, and belonging. As a result, many consumers end up associating branded goods with personal worth and validation.

The fear of missing out is strong on social media, where people constantly see others enjoying the latest products or experiences. This "highlight reel" of other people's lives can make us feel like we're falling behind, pressuring us to buy things we don't truly need. FOMO-driven spending is often impulsive and can lead to regret, especially when the purchase doesn't bring the expected happiness.

Overcoming the influence of advertising and FOMO requires developing a sense of self-awareness and understanding that our worth isn't determined by the items we own. Recognizing these psychological tactics can help reduce impulsive spending and enable a more balanced relationship with luxury.

5. Cultivating a Healthy Relationship with Luxury

To break free from the mental and financial toll of comparison culture, it's essential to cultivate a healthy relationship with luxury. This involves shifting from external validation to internal fulfillment, focusing on personal values and priorities rather than societal expectations. Here are some strategies to help you foster a positive mindset:

- **Limit Social Media Exposure**: Consider reducing your time on social media platforms that amplify comparison, or unfollow accounts that trigger feelings of inadequacy. Focus on connecting with content that inspires growth and positivity rather than materialism.

- **Practice Gratitude**: Regularly reflecting on the things you're grateful for can help shift your focus from what you lack to what you have. Practicing gratitude has been shown to improve mental well-being, helping you feel more content and less inclined to seek validation through luxury items.

- **Set Personal Goals**: Define what truly matters to you and set goals aligned with those values. You're less likely to feel the need to conform to external expectations or compare yourself to others, when you have a clear vision of your priorities.

- **Embrace Minimalism**: Simplifying your life by embracing minimalism can help reduce the urge to buy unnecessary items. Minimalism encourages mindful consumption, allowing you to focus on what adds genuine value to your life.

- **Focus on Experiences Over Things**: Prioritizing experiences over material goods can foster a deeper sense of happiness. Studies have shown that experiences, such as spending time with loved ones or pursuing personal passions, contribute to lasting well-being.

By implementing these strategies, you can develop a more balanced approach to luxury and reduce the impact of comparison culture on your mental health.

Key Takeaways

Comparison culture can lead to a cycle of dissatisfaction, where people constantly seek validation through luxury purchases. Here are some key takeaways from this chapter:

1. **Social media Amplifies Comparison**: Constant exposure to luxury on social media can trigger feelings of inadequacy and drive impulsive consumption.
2. **Happiness From Luxury is Temporary**: The "hedonic treadmill" explains why the happiness derived from material goods is short-lived, often leading to a cycle of repeated spending.
3. **Financial Stress affects Mental Health**: The strain of keeping up with luxury culture can lead to debt, anxiety, and reduced well-being.
4. **Advertising Exploits FOMO**: Advertising fuels the desire for luxury by creating a fear of missing out, making consumers believe they need branded items for validation.
5. **Healthy Alternatives to Luxury Consumption**: Practices like gratitude, minimalism, and focusing on experiences over things can foster a more fulfilling relationship with material possessions.

Final Reflection

In a world where comparison is constant, finding contentment requires looking inward. Luxury should be about enhancing one's life, not about creating stress, debt, or dissatisfaction. By cultivating self-awareness and focusing on what truly matters, we can break free from the pressures of comparison culture and embrace a healthier, more fulfilling relationship with luxury.

True luxury lies not in brands or possessions but in the peace, purpose, and joy that comes from living authentically. As you continue your journey, remember that lasting happiness comes from within, not from comparing yourself to others.

End of Part IV: The Ethical and Psychological Trap of Luxury Goods

Part IV examined the ethical and psychological effects of luxury consumerism, focusing on how brands manipulate consumers' emotions and self-perceptions. This part highlighted the mental and social costs of chasing branded goods. Key takeaways are:

1. **Walking Billboards**: Branded goods turn people into advertisements, often reducing personal expression to a mere display of logos and labels.
2. **Exploitation of Human Nature**: Brands capitalize on deep-seated desires for recognition and status, creating a never-ending cycle of consumption and dissatisfaction.
3. **Mental Health Impacts**: The pressures of comparison culture, fueled by social media, can lead to stress, anxiety, and reduced self-esteem, creating a hidden psychological cost of luxury consumption.
4. **Financial and Social Consequences**: Luxury spending can strain personal finances, affecting mental health and leading to social issues like debt and interpersonal stress.

PART V

THE PROS AND CONS OF LUXURY GOODS

Chapter 17

The Middle-Class Illusion – Trapped in the Branded Goods Cycle

Manoj, a middle-class man from Jaipur, once prided himself on his ability to save and plan for the future. He had a steady job, a comfortable home, and a family he cherished. But over time, he began noticing something. His friends, colleagues, and even distant relatives were buying things he couldn't afford — luxury cars, branded clothes, expensive phones. Slowly, he began feeling left out. He wasn't sure when it happened, but suddenly he found himself caught in a new reality: **the middle-class illusion.**

This illusion is one that many middle-class families in India find themselves trapped in — the idea that buying branded goods, owning luxury items, and living like the wealthy will bring happiness, satisfaction, and validation. The problem is, this illusion rarely delivers on its promise. Instead, it creates a cycle of debt, dissatisfaction, and a never-ending chase for more.

In this chapter, we will explore how the middle class gets trapped in the **branded goods cycle**, constantly seeking validation and superiority through material possessions. We'll look at the psychological and economic consequences of this cycle and how to break free from it, finding fulfillment outside of consumerism.

The Middle-Class Hunger for More

For many middle-class families, there is a **constant hunger for more.** This hunger is driven by a mix of societal pressures, economic aspirations, and the desire to move up the social ladder. Middle-class families often find themselves in a delicate balance — they've moved beyond the financial struggles of the lower class, but they're still far from the comfort and wealth of the upper class. Branded goods, in many ways, represent the bridge between these two worlds.

Owning a luxury car, wearing branded clothes, or using the latest smartphone are not just about personal enjoyment for the middle class. They are about **signaling success.** These items become symbols of hard work, achievements, and upward mobility. For Manoj, buying a luxury watch wasn't about telling the time — it was about telling the world that he had made it, that he belonged in a higher social circle.

Middle-class culture deeply embeds this aspirational mindset. Unlike the wealthy, who can buy luxury goods without thinking twice, the middle class often sees these purchases as rewards for their hard work or as symbols of their success. But the problem arises when this mindset spirals into a cycle of constant consumption, where the need to keep up with others leads to financial strain and emotional exhaustion.

Debt and Financial Strain: The Hidden Costs of Keeping Up

For many middle-class families, the pursuit of branded goods leads to one inevitable consequence: **debt**. The financial strain of buying luxury items often forces people to take out loans, use credit cards, or dip into their savings. While this might provide temporary satisfaction, the long-term impact can be devastating.

Manoj experienced this firsthand. After purchasing a luxury car on an EMI plan, he felt proud every time he drove it around town. But the monthly payments quickly became a source of stress. His family's budget was already tight, and the car payments pushed them to the edge. Soon, Manoj had to cut back on other expenses, like saving for his children's education and planning for family vacations.

This is the reality for many working-class families. The pursuit of luxury often leads to **financial instability**, as people prioritize branded goods over long-term financial security. What begins as an effort to fit in or signal success turns into a burden, with debt piling up and the stress of meeting payments becoming overwhelming.

The Emotional Toll of the Branded Goods Cycle

While the financial strain of owning branded goods is significant, the **emotional toll** is often just as damaging. The middle-class illusion promises happiness, confidence, and social acceptance through material possessions, but these goods rarely deliver on that promise. Instead, they create a cycle of **dissatisfaction.**

Manoj's initial excitement about owning a luxury car faded quickly. After a few months, the car became just another part of his routine. It no longer brought him the same joy or sense of pride. However, instead of recognizing that branded goods wouldn't bring him lasting happiness, he began looking for the next item to buy. A new phone, a branded watch, or a designer suit — the chase for more never stopped.

This is the psychological trap of the branded goods cycle. The middle class often falls into the belief that each new purchase will bring fulfillment, but the satisfaction is always short-lived. This results in continuous consumption, with the desire for more replacing the satisfaction of what has been obtained.

Why the Middle Class Feels Trapped?

One reason the working class feels so trapped in this cycle is that social media, in particular, has amplified the effect of constantly comparing themselves to others. Every day, people are bombarded with images of friends, colleagues, and even strangers flaunting their branded goods, luxury vacations, and new purchases. The curated perfection of these posts creates a sense of inadequacy, pushing people to **keep up** with what they see online.

For the middle class, societal pressures compound this sense of inadequacy. In India, where social status is often measured by material possessions, the pressure to own branded goods is immense. Whether it's attending a wedding, a family function, or a corporate event, people feel the need to dress in the latest fashion, drive the newest cars, and carry the trendiest gadgets.

This creates a **vicious cycle**. The more people compare themselves to others, the more they feel the need to buy branded goods. And the more they buy, the more they feel trapped in a cycle of debt, dissatisfaction, and constant consumption.

Breaking Free from the Illusion

The first step to breaking free from the branded goods cycle is to **recognize the illusion.** Branded goods, luxury items, and material possessions may bring temporary satisfaction, but they will never provide lasting happiness or fulfillment. The middle-class illusion falsely ties status and success to what we own, when in reality, they are tied to how we live.

Here are a few strategies to help break free from the cycle:

1. **Shift Your Focus to Experiences:** Research shows that experiences, rather than material possessions, bring more long-term happiness. Instead of spending money on branded goods, invest in experiences that create memories and enrich your life, such as travel, learning new skills, or spending time with loved ones.

2. **Reassess Your Values:** Take a step back and ask yourself what truly matters to you. Is it financial security, personal growth, or relationships? Align your spending habits with these values and resist the pressure to buy things that don't bring meaningful value to your life.

3. **Challenge Social Comparisons:** Social media and societal pressures can make it easy to fall into the trap of comparing yourself to others. But remember, everyone's journey is different. Focus on your own goals and achievements, and avoid the constant comparisons that fuel the desire for more.

4. **Prioritize Financial Health:** Financial freedom brings more peace of mind than any branded item ever could. Make a commitment to prioritize your financial health by saving for the future, paying off debt, and investing in long-term goals. The

satisfaction of financial security far outweighs the fleeting joy of a luxury purchase.

Conclusion: The Path to True Fulfillment

Breaking free from the middle-class illusion requires a **shift in mindset**. It's about recognizing that true fulfillment doesn't come from branded goods, but from living a life aligned with your values, goals, and relationships. For Manoj, this realization came after years of chasing after luxury items that never brought him the happiness he expected. Once he began focusing on what truly mattered — his family, his financial security, and his personal growth — he found a sense of peace that no branded good could provide.

You don't have to remain trapped in the cycle of branded goods. By shifting our focus away from material possessions and toward experiences, personal fulfillment, and financial security, we can break free from the illusion and create a life that brings lasting happiness.

Chapter 18

The New Upscale Market Platforms – How the Digital Age Fuels Aspirational Buying

In the past, luxury and branded goods were accessible only through exclusive boutiques and high-end stores located in metropolitan cities. Today, however, the rise of **upscale market platforms** has made luxury goods more accessible to the middle class. With just a few clicks, anyone can browse, compare, and purchase branded items from the comfort of their home. While this digital transformation has democratized access to luxury, it has also intensified the pressure on consumers to buy more, keep up with trends, and indulge in aspirational buying.

In this chapter, we will explore the role of **online upscale market platforms** in fueling the desire for branded goods. We will examine how these platforms shape consumer behavior, how they capitalize on the middle class's aspirations, and how their marketing strategies make luxury goods feel more attainable — even if they come at a financial cost. We'll also discuss how consumers can navigate these platforms responsibly without falling into the trap of overspending.

The Rise of Upscale Market Platforms

Over the past decade, upscale market platforms like Tata CLiQ Luxury, Nykaa Luxe, Amazon Luxury, and other high-end e-commerce websites have transformed the way people shop for branded goods. What once required a trip to an elite boutique in a five-star hotel can now be accessed from any smartphone or laptop. These platforms offer an array of luxury items — from designer handbags to high-end watches, premium clothing, and branded electronics — all available with the click of a button.

This shift has made luxury goods more **accessible** than ever before. No longer confined to physical stores of cities like Mumbai or Delhi, consumers from smaller towns and cities can now indulge in branded shopping online. This has opened the doors for working-class individuals to explore the world of luxury, fueling their desire to own branded goods.

Personalization Through AI and Data Analytics

One of the most significant ways technology has enhanced luxury shopping is through personalization. AI-driven algorithms and data analytics have transformed how consumers interact with brands, making the shopping experience more tailored and convenient.

Luxury e-commerce platforms and brands now use sophisticated algorithms to track consumer behavior, preferences, and past purchases. Based on this data, they provide personalized recommendations, showing products that are more likely to appeal to individual shoppers. For example, if someone frequently browses for handbags on a luxury platform, the next time they visit, the website will highlight similar handbags or offer deals on specific brands.

This level of personalization creates a customized shopping experience, making consumers feel that the brand understands their unique preferences. For middle-class consumers, this tailored approach enhances their shopping experience, encouraging them to make repeat purchases and feel more connected to the brand.

In addition, targeted advertisements based on browsing history or social media activity reinforce this personalization. When consumers see ads for products they've recently searched for, they're more likely to click through and make a purchase. This technology-driven personalization blurs the line between casual browsing and intentional shopping, making it easier for consumers to buy luxury goods on impulse.

Virtual Try-Ons and Augmented Reality (AR)

Another technological innovation that has transformed the luxury shopping experience is the use of virtual try-ons and augmented reality (AR). For years, one of the key advantages of shopping in physical stores was the ability to try on items before making a purchase. However, technology has now made it possible to replicate that experience online.

Many luxury fashion and beauty brands have incorporated virtual try-on technology into their websites and apps. For example, consumers can now use their smartphones or computers to virtually try on clothing, accessories, or makeup, seeing how a product will look on them without ever leaving their home. Some beauty brands offer virtual makeup tools that allow users to try different shades of lipstick, foundation, or eyeshadow using their device's camera.

Augmented reality mirrors in stores and online platforms allow customers to visualize how products will look in real life. Whether it's trying on sunglasses, jewelry, or even luxury watches, these tools have revolutionized the shopping experience by bridging the gap between physical and digital shopping. This immersive experience increases the likelihood of purchase because consumers can better visualize how the item will fit into their lives.

This technology provides a valuable alternative for middle-class consumers who may not have easy access to high-end luxury boutiques. It allows them to experience the luxury shopping process in a more interactive way, making the experience feel more real and satisfying. In many ways, it has democratized access to luxury, offering the middle class a similar experience to what they would get in store, but in a digital format.

The Impact of AI-Driven Customer Support

Another technological advancement that has enhanced the luxury shopping experience is the use of AI-driven customer support. Many luxury e-commerce platforms now use chatbots and AI-powered virtual assistants to provide 24/7 customer service, answering questions about products, assisting with purchases, and helping with returns.

These AI tools make the shopping experience more efficient and personalized. Instead of waiting for a customer service representative, consumers can get instant answers to their questions, improving their overall experience with the brand. This level of convenience is particularly important for middle-class shoppers who may need guidance when purchasing high-end items.

Moreover, AI-driven support can help consumers find the right products based on their preferences and past purchases. For example, a virtual assistant might recommend a new collection of handbags based on a customer's previous shopping behavior, creating a more curated and satisfying experience.

Aspirational Buying in the Digital Age

One of the main reasons upscale market platforms have gained popularity is their ability to tap into **aspirational buying** — the act of purchasing items that represent a higher social status or lifestyle than what one currently has. In the past, the exclusivity of luxury goods made them difficult to access for many middle-class consumers. But now, with these digital platforms, the gap between aspiration and access has significantly narrowed.

For example, Raj, a 32-year-old software engineer from Pune, often browses upscale platforms to see the latest designer shoes and watches. Even though he might not need a new pair of shoes, the aspirational allure of owning something premium drives him to add items to his cart. The promise of **next-day delivery**, easy **EMI options**, and **seasonal discounts** makes these purchases feel more affordable and attainable. Raj ends up spending more than he intended, driven by the feeling that he deserves to own these luxury items.

This phenomenon is common among working-class consumers. The availability of luxury goods online creates a sense of **immediacy** and **gratification,** leading people to make impulsive decisions in pursuit of the lifestyle they aspire to.

How Online Platforms Influence Consumer Behavior

Upscale market platforms have features that not only make luxury goods accessible but also encourage **constant engagement** and **frequent purchases**. Some tactics these platforms use to influence consumer behavior include:

1. **Personalized Recommendations:** By analyzing browsing history and purchase behavior, these platforms provide personalized product recommendations that are tailored to the consumer's preferences. This increases the likelihood of making repeat purchases, as consumers tend to perceive that the platform understands their tastes and desires.

2. **Flash Sales and Limited-Time Offers:** One of the most effective ways to create urgency is through **flash sales** and **limited-time offers**. These promotions make consumers feel like they are getting a great deal, even if they are spending more than they had planned. The fear of missing out (FOMO) drives impulsive buying.

3. **EMI and Buy Now, Pay Later Options:** Platforms that offer **easy financing options**, such as EMI plans or "buy now, pay later" schemes, make it easier for consumers to purchase luxury items without feeling the financial burden upfront. This, however, can lead to debt accumulation as consumers overspend on items they can't afford outright.

4. **Free Returns and Refunds:** The promise of easy returns and refunds reduces the risk of making a luxury purchase, as consumers feel that they can always change their mind later. This encourages more frequent buying, as shoppers feel more confident in their purchasing decisions.

5. **Exclusive Offers for Members:** Many upscale platforms offer membership programs or loyalty rewards that give consumers access to exclusive sales, early product launches, or additional discounts. This sense of exclusivity makes consumers feel like

they are part of a special group, reinforcing the idea that they are engaging in a premium experience.

These strategies **maximize sales** by keeping consumers engaged, excited, and always looking for their next purchase.

Mobile Apps and On-the-Go Shopping

The rise of **mobile apps** has further revolutionized luxury shopping. Most luxury brands and marketplaces now offer dedicated apps that allow users to shop on the go. These apps are designed to provide a seamless shopping experience, with features like personalized recommendations, real-time notifications about sales or new arrivals, and exclusive app-only offers.

For middle-class consumers who are often busy balancing work and family life, these apps make luxury shopping more convenient. Whether they're commuting to work, waiting in line, or relaxing at home, they can browse and buy luxury goods whenever and wherever they want. This convenience has made mobile apps a popular tool for middle-class shoppers, who may not have the time to visit physical stores or sit down at a computer to make purchases.

Moreover, mobile apps often incorporate **push notifications**, alerting users about limited-time deals or reminding them about items left in their shopping cart. These reminders create a sense of urgency and encourage impulse buying, which can be particularly effective in the context of luxury goods.

The Trap of "Affordable Luxury"

One of the most dangerous aspects of online upscale platforms is the concept of **"affordable luxury."** While traditional luxury brands like Louis Vuitton or Chanel remain out of reach for most middle-class consumers, many platforms feature mid-range brands that offer the appearance of luxury at a more accessible price point. These brands position themselves as offering high-quality, stylish products that mimic the aesthetics of luxury goods — but at a fraction of the price.

This creates the illusion that luxury is **within reach** for the middle class. Consumers who might not be able to afford a ₹5 lakh handbag can still buy into the luxury lifestyle by purchasing a ₹15,000 designer purse or a ₹10,000 branded watch. However, this can lead to a **pattern of overspending**, as people try to maintain the appearance of a luxury lifestyle without the financial means to support it.

For working-class individuals like Raj, this pattern often results in **frequent purchases of mid-range luxury items** that drain savings and create financial stress. While each individual purchase might seem affordable, the cumulative effect can be significant, leaving consumers with little financial security.

Balancing Aspirational Buying with Financial Responsibility

While upscale market platforms make luxury more accessible, it's important for middle-class consumers to approach these platforms with **caution** and **financial discipline**. Here are a few strategies to help balance the desire for luxury with responsible spending:

1. **Set a Budget for Luxury Purchases:** Before browsing an upscale platform, set a clear budget for how much you're willing to spend on luxury items. Stick to this budget and avoid being swayed by discounts or flash sales.
2. **Avoid Impulse Buying:** One of the most common traps on upscale platforms is the impulse purchase. Take a step back before making a purchase and ask yourself if the item is something you truly need or if you're being influenced by marketing tactics.
3. **Limit the Use of EMI and Credit Options:** While EMI options make luxury purchases seem more affordable, they can lead to

debt accumulation over time. Try to limit the use of credit and pay upfront for purchases.

4. **Prioritize Quality Over Quantity:** Instead of buying several mid-range luxury items, consider investing in fewer high-quality pieces that will last longer and provide greater value. This helps avoid the cycle of constantly upgrading or replacing items.

5. **Focus on Financial Goals:** Ensure that your luxury purchases don't come at the expense of your long-term financial goals, such as saving for retirement, emergency funds, or investing in experiences that bring lasting value.

Conclusion: Navigating the Upscale Market Mindfully

Upscale market platforms have transformed the way middle-class consumers access luxury goods, offering convenience, variety, and the allure of aspirational buying. However, it's essential to recognize the **psychological tactics** and **economic pressures** at play. These platforms are designed to create a sense of urgency, desire, and status – but falling into the trap of overspending can lead to financial strain and dissatisfaction.

For consumers like Raj, learning to navigate upscale platforms mindfully is key to avoiding the pitfalls of aspirational buying. By setting clear boundaries, focusing on long-term financial goals, and resisting the pressure to keep up with trends, it's possible to enjoy the benefits of luxury without sacrificing financial stability.

End of Part V: The Pros and Cons of Luxury Goods

In Part V, we discussed both the benefits and drawbacks of branded items, offering a balanced perspective on luxury. This part encourages readers to understand when luxury items might add genuine value and when they might simply add unnecessary stress. Key takeaways include:

1. **Quality and Craftsmanship**: Luxury items often offer exceptional quality, making them a worthwhile investment for those seeking durability and lasting value.
2. **Middle-Class Illusions**: The middle class may pursue luxury items to "belong" or to project status, which can lead to a cycle of stress and financial strain.
3. **Impact of Digital Platforms**: The internet and social media have amplified the visibility of luxury lifestyles, intensifying social pressure and creating a more public sphere for luxury consumption.
4. **Knowing When Luxury Makes Sense**: Not all luxury is superficial—certain items provide real benefits and can be enjoyed in moderation, provided they resonate with personal values and goals.

PART VI

BREAKING FREE AND FINDING REAL VALUE

<h1 style="text-align:center">Chapter 19</h1>

The Pros and Cons of Branded Goods for the Middle Class

Branded goods have a special allure for many people, particularly those in the working class. They represent success, prestige, and the desire for a better lifestyle. But while branded items can bring satisfaction and even long-term value, they also come with significant downsides. The middle class often finds itself caught between the excitement of owning luxury goods and the reality of the financial pressures that come with them.

In this chapter, we'll inspect both the **pros** and **cons** of branded goods for middle-class consumers. By understanding both sides, readers can make more informed decisions about their purchases and strike a balance between enjoying luxury and maintaining financial well-being.

The Pros of Branded Goods for the Middle Class

1. Quality and Durability

One of the primary reasons people choose branded goods over cheaper alternatives is the **quality** they offer. Well-established brands often use high-quality materials and superior craftsmanship, resulting in products that are more durable and reliable.

For example, when you purchase a pair of branded leather shoes, you're not just paying for the logo — you're paying for craftsmanship that ensures the shoes last longer, remain comfortable, and maintain their appearance over time. In contrast, non-branded products, while cheaper initially, may wear out more quickly, leading to repeated purchases and high long-term costs.

2. Emotional Satisfaction

There's an undeniable **emotional appeal** to owning a luxury or branded item. For many middle-class consumers, buying a branded product represents a reward for hard work or a milestone in life. Whether it's the pride of owning a well-made watch or the confidence that comes from wearing designer clothes, branded goods can provide a sense of personal satisfaction that goes beyond their utility.

Consider Aarti, a middle-class woman from Delhi. After receiving a promotion at work, she decided to invest in a luxury handbag she had been dreaming of. For Aarti, the handbag wasn't just an accessory — it was a symbol of her achievement and a reward for her years of dedication. The emotional satisfaction she derived from this purchase made it worth the investment.

3. Status and Social Perception

Many cultures, including India, associate owning branded goods with social status. Branded items often serve as markers of success and upward mobility. For working-class consumers, owning a luxury car, wearing a designer watch, or carrying a high-end handbag can signal to others that they've "made it." This social recognition can boost self-esteem and improve one's standing in both professional and personal circles.

4. Investment Potential

Certain branded goods — particularly luxury items like watches, jewelry, and high-end handbags — can actually **appreciate in value** over time. Collectible watches from brands like Rolex, limited-edition designer handbags, or fine jewelry often increase in worth, making them not just purchases but **investments**. For middle-class consumers who handpick high-quality branded items, these products can provide both emotional satisfaction and financial returns.

The Cons of Branded Goods for the Middle Class

1. Financial Strain

While branded goods can offer high quality, they often come with a **hefty price tag** that many middle-class consumers struggle to afford. The cost of owning luxury items can lead to **financial strain**, especially if bought impulsively on credit. For families trying to save for long-term goals like education, retirement, or home ownership, spending large amounts on branded goods can divert resources away from more important financial priorities.

Take Rakesh, a middle-class man from Hyderabad, who bought a luxury car on an EMI plan. While the car brought him temporary satisfaction, the monthly payments became a burden, leaving him with less money for household expenses and savings. Eventually, the financial stress outweighed the joy of owning the car.

2. Short-Lived Satisfaction

One of the biggest challenges with branded goods is that the **happiness they bring is often short-lived.** The excitement of owning a new luxury item fades over time, and consumers look for the next new product. This leads to a cycle of **continuous consumption,** where people are always chasing the next branded item to feel satisfied.

This psychological phenomenon, known as **hedonic adaptation,** explains that even the most expensive items lose their emotional impact after a while. For middle-class consumers, this can lead to frustration and dissatisfaction, as they realize that branded goods don't bring the lasting happiness they expected.

3. Social Pressure and Comparison

The middle class is often caught in a cycle of **social comparison,** driven by the desire to keep up with peers, colleagues, or relatives who own branded goods. This pressure can lead to overspending, as people feel the need to buy luxury items simply to maintain their social standing. Social media has amplified this effect, with users constantly seeing others flaunting their latest purchases.

For example, Neha, a working-class woman from Mumbai, who started feeling inadequate after seeing her friends post pictures of their luxury vacations and branded clothes on Instagram. Even though Neha was financially stable, the pressure to keep up led her to overspend on branded items she didn't need, pushing her budget to its limits.

4. Debt Accumulation

One of the most significant downsides of buying branded goods is the risk of **debt accumulation**. Many middle-class consumers finance luxury purchases through **credit cards, EMI plans**, or **personal loans**, creating a financial burden that can take months or even years to repay. This debt not only causes financial stress but can also damage long-term financial health by diverting money away from savings and investments.

Suresh, a working-class man from Bengaluru, used a credit card to purchase a high-end smartphone. While he enjoyed the prestige of owning the latest model, the interest charges on his credit card soon added up, leaving him with an enormous debt that took years to pay off.

Striking a Balance: How to Enjoy Branded Goods Responsibly

While branded goods can offer significant value in certain situations, it's important for middle-class consumers to approach luxury purchases with **financial responsibility**. Here are a few strategies for striking a balance between enjoying luxury items and maintaining financial well-being:

1. **Prioritize Financial Health:** Before making any luxury purchase, ensure that your essential financial goals — such as saving for retirement, emergency funds, and debt repayment — are in order. Avoid sacrificing long-term security for short-term satisfaction.

2. **Save for Big Purchases:** Instead of buying branded goods impulsively or on credit, take the time to **save up** for luxury items. This not only helps you avoid debt, but also makes the purchase more rewarding once you've reached your goal.

3. **Invest in Timeless, High-Quality Pieces:** If you choose to buy branded goods, focus on items that are **durable** and **timeless.** Avoid chasing trends and instead invest in products that will last for years and provide long-term value.

4. **Limit the Use of Credit:** If possible, avoid financing luxury purchases with credit or EMI plans, which can lead to debt accumulation. Paying upfront for branded goods helps you stay within your budget and reduces the financial burden.

Conclusion: Weighing the Pros and Cons of Branded Goods

For middle-class consumers, branded goods offer both **benefits** and **challenges**. While they can bring quality, emotional satisfaction, and social recognition, they can also lead to financial strain, debt, and short-lived happiness. The key to enjoying branded goods responsibly is to approach these purchases mindfully, ensuring that they align with your long-term financial goals and personal values.

By understanding both the pros and cons of branded goods, middle-class consumers can make more informed decisions and find a balance between indulging in luxury and maintaining financial well-being

Chapter 20

How Brands Exploit Human Nature – The Hidden Psychology Behind Consumerism

From flashy advertisements to subtle marketing messages, brands have mastered the art of tapping into human psychology to drive consumer behavior. They know that our purchasing decisions are not always logical or based purely on necessity; deep-seated desires, emotional triggers, and social conditioning often influence them. The working class, in particular, is a prime target for this type of psychological manipulation, as they are constantly seeking validation, success, and the sense of "having made it."

In this chapter, we will dive deep into how brands exploit **human nature** to fuel consumerism. By understanding these psychological triggers, readers can become more aware of how brands influence their decisions and learn to make more mindful, intentional choices about what they buy.

The Power of Emotional Marketing

One of the most effective tools in a brand's arsenal is **emotional marketing**. Rather than simply selling a product's features, brands craft stories and images that evoke emotions like happiness, nostalgia, confidence, or even fear. This emotional connection often leads consumers to buy products not because they need them, but because they want to feel a certain way.

For example, think about a luxury perfume advertisement. The commercial doesn't just show the bottle and list its ingredients — it portrays a glamorous lifestyle, with a confident, attractive person walking through an upscale party, capturing everyone's attention. The underlying message is that by using this perfume, you can feel as confident and desirable as the person in the ad. It's not about the fragrance itself; it's about the **emotion** the brand is selling.

This tactic is especially effective towards working-class consumers who are seeking to elevate their status or gain recognition. Branded goods often promise to fill an emotional void — whether that's the need to feel successful, admired, or happy. The key here is that brands are not selling products; they are selling **feelings**.

Scarcity and FOMO: Creating a Sense of Urgency

Another powerful psychological tactic used by brands is the **scarcity principle**. By creating a sense of urgency — such as limited-edition releases or "while supplies last" sales — brands trigger a fear of missing out (FOMO) in consumers. This scarcity makes the product seem more valuable, and consumers are more likely to make impulsive decisions to buy before it's too late.

Luxury brands often use scarcity to maintain an aura of exclusivity. By limiting the availability of their products, brands make consumers feel that owning the item will set them apart from others. For middle-class buyers, this tactic can be very persuasive, as it taps into their desire to signal success and differentiate themselves from their peers.

Consider how brands like Nike or Apple launch new products. Whether it's a limited-edition sneaker or the latest iPhone, the message is simple: buy it now, or you'll miss out. This creates a sense of urgency that overrides rational thinking. Middle-class consumers, eager to keep up with trends and signal their status, often feel compelled to make the purchase, even if they can't afford it.

Social Proof: The Influence of Others

Social proof is another psychological tool that brands use to drive consumer behavior. It's the idea that people are more likely to do something if they see others doing it. Brands leverage this by showcasing influencers, celebrities, and even ordinary people using their products, creating the impression that the product is widely accepted and admired.

In the age of social media, this tactic has become even more powerful. When people see their favorite influencer or celebrity using a branded item, they're more likely to want it for themselves. Middle-class consumers, in particular, are susceptible to this kind of influence, as they often look to others to determine what is considered fashionable, trendy, or socially acceptable.

For example, imagine a young professional in Mumbai scrolling through Instagram and seeing multiple posts of influencers wearing the same designer bag. The posts feature happy, successful-looking people enjoying glamorous lifestyles. This repeated exposure creates the impression that owning the bag is a sign of success, prompting the viewer to desire the same lifestyle and purchase the product.

The Desire for Superiority: Brands as Status Symbols

One of the most deeply rooted aspects of human nature that brands exploit is the **desire for superiority**. People have an inherent need to feel important, successful, and above others. Luxury brands capitalize on this by positioning their products as **status symbols**, making consumers believe that owning these items will elevate them in the eyes of others.

For middle-class consumers who are often striving to improve their social standing, branded goods offer an opportunity to signal their success and achievement. Whether it's a high-end watch, a luxury car, or a designer outfit, these items serve as markers of success and social distinction.

The problem with this, however, is that pursuit of status through material possessions often leads to **Emotional Exhaustion**. The satisfaction of owning a branded item is usually short-lived, as people quickly adapt to their new possession and begin seeking the next product that will make them feel superior. This cycle of consumption keeps people trapped in a constant pursuit of validation, without ever bringing true contentment.

Anchoring and Pricing: Why Luxury Feels Worth It?

Brands also use the psychological concept of **Anchoring** to manipulate how consumers perceive the value of their products. Anchoring occurs when people rely heavily on the first piece of information they receive — in this case, the price of a product — to make subsequent judgments. By setting high prices for their goods, luxury brands create the perception that their products are inherently valuable.

For example, when a high-end fashion brand releases a handbag with a price tag of ₹2 lakh, that price becomes the "anchor" in the consumer's mind. Even if the consumer cannot afford the handbag, they will start comparing other products against this price point. Suddenly, a ₹50,000 handbag from another luxury brand seems more reasonable, even though it is still well beyond what the consumer can comfortably afford.

This pricing strategy plays on the middle-class desire for **affordable luxury,** making them feel that they are getting a good deal on a prestigious item. However, this perceived value is often an illusion, and consumers end up spending more than they intended.

The Halo Effect: When One Product Enhances the Brand's Image

The **Halo Effect** occurs when the positive impression of one product enhances the perception of the entire brand. Luxury brands use this effect to their advantage by producing high-quality flagship products that create a positive association with the rest of their offerings. Consumers who had a pleasant experience with one branded item are more likely to believe that all products from the same brand are of equally high quality, even if they haven't tried them.

For instance, a middle-class consumer might buy a luxury perfume and be extremely satisfied with its quality and packaging. Because of this positive experience, they trust the brand and are more inclined to buy other items from the brand, such as watches, handbags, or clothing, believing that they are all of the same high standard.

This brand loyalty can be beneficial in some cases, but it can also lead to **blind trust**, where consumers overlook better, more affordable alternatives simply because they are loyal to a particular brand.

Breaking Free from Psychological Traps

Understanding the psychological tactics that brands use is the first step in breaking free from **consumer manipulation**. Here are some strategies to help middle-class consumers resist the pressure to buy into branded goods:

1. **Recognize Emotional Triggers:** Before making a purchase, ask yourself why you're drawn to the item. Are you buying it because it fulfills a need, or are you being influenced by emotions like envy, insecurity, or fear of missing out?

2. **Resist Impulse Buying:** Many luxury purchases are made on impulse, driven by the emotional tactics used by brands. Take a step back, give yourself time to think, and reconsider whether the purchase is worth the financial and emotional cost.

3. **Question the Value:** Just because a product is expensive doesn't mean it's valuable. Challenge the perception of luxury by asking whether the product offers long-term value or is simply priced high to create an aura of exclusivity.

4. **Focus on Personal Goals:** Remember that branded goods are not a measure of success or fulfillment. Focus on your own personal and financial goals rather than seeking validation through material possessions.

5. **Limit Social Media Influence:** social media often amplifies the desire for branded goods by creating a culture of comparison. Reduce exposure to influencers or accounts that make you feel inadequate or trigger unnecessary spending.

Conclusion: Understanding and Overcoming Brand Influence

Brands are experts at exploiting human nature to drive consumer behavior, using emotional marketing, social proof, and psychological tactics to sell their products. For working-class consumers, recognizing these strategies is key to breaking free from the cycle of aspirational buying and making more intentional, mindful purchasing decisions.

By understanding the hidden psychology behind consumerism, people can reclaim control over their choices, focusing on what truly matters rather than falling into the trap of luxury brands. The power lies in recognizing that true success and happiness come from within, not from the products we own.

Chapter 21

The Paradox of Choice – Does More Really Make Us Happier?

In today's consumer-driven world, there is an overwhelming amount of choice. We constantly face decisions about what to buy, wear, or own, with hundreds of smartphone models and thousands of clothing brands vying for our attention. On the surface, it may seem that more choice leads to greater happiness, allowing us to select products that perfectly match our needs and desires. However, research and real-world experience show that **too much choice** can lead to **stress, dissatisfaction, and even paralysis.**

The working class is increasingly exposed to luxury brands, upscale platforms, and a variety of product options, the abundance of choice can be a double-edged sword. While it offers the promise of better, more customized products, it also creates pressure, confusion, and anxiety over making the "right" decision.

In this chapter, we will explore the **paradox of choice** — the idea that more options don't necessarily lead to more happiness. We'll examine how having too many choices affects consumer behavior, especially in the middle class, and how simplifying our decision-making process can lead to greater satisfaction and peace of mind.

The Psychology Behind Choice Overload

One of the most significant challenges of modern consumerism is **Choice Overload.** As the number of options increases, the decision-making process becomes more complex and overwhelming. This phenomenon has been extensively studied by psychologists, who have found that having too many choices can lead to **decision fatigue, regret,** and **anxiety.**

For example, imagine walking into a luxury electronics store to buy a new smartphone. Instead of being presented with a few models, you're faced with dozens of options, each with slightly distinct features, prices, and brand names. While the variety might initially seem appealing, comparing all these options can become exhausting. You might start second-guessing your choices, wondering if you're missing out on a better deal or if the product you choose will truly meet your needs.

This **paralysis by analysis** leads to **decision fatigue**, where the mental energy required to evaluate each option becomes overwhelming. Instead of enjoying the process of buying something new, you're left feeling confused, stressed, and even more uncertain than when you started.

The Paradox of Choice: More Isn't Always Better

The **Paradox of Choice** is the idea that while having options can increase freedom, too many options can reduce happiness and satisfaction. This concept was popularized by psychologist Barry Schwartz in his book *The Paradox of Choice*, where he argued that when we are faced with an abundance of choices, we become **less happy** with our decisions, even if the outcome is objectively good.

This paradox is especially relevant for branded goods and luxury items. As upscale market platforms and luxury brands offer more and more choices, middle-class consumers are faced with the challenge of making the "perfect" decision. Should you buy the latest smartphone from a premium brand, or is a mid-range brand good enough? Should you choose a designer outfit for a family wedding, or go with something more affordable?

These decisions are complicated by the **fear of missing out** (FOMO) — the worry that by choosing one product, you're missing out on something better. This fear, combined with the pressure to make the "right" choice, often leads to **buyer's remorse**, where consumers regret their decision after the purchase is made.

The Impact on the Middle Class

For the working class, the paradox of choice is challenging because they are caught between **budget constraints** and the desire to own luxury items. The abundance of choices — whether it's between a high-end branded good and a mid-range alternative or between different financing options — creates a **sense of pressure** to make the most out of every purchase.

Consider Ritu, a middle-class woman from Jaipur. When it came time to buy a new refrigerator, she spent weeks comparing different models online, reading reviews, and visiting multiple stores. With so many options available — from budget brands to premium models — Ritu became overwhelmed by the sheer number of features, prices, and offers. Instead of feeling excited about her purchase, she felt stressed, anxious, and drained by the decision-making process.

This experience is common for many middle-class consumers who feel the need to **optimize** every purchase, particularly when it involves significant financial investment. The fear of making the wrong choice, combined with the pressure to find the best value for money, can make the shopping experience more stressful than enjoyable.

The Downsides of More Choice: Regret, Dissatisfaction, and Stress

When faced with too many choices, middle-class consumers are more likely to experience **regret** after making a purchase. Even if the product they choose meets their needs, they may continue to wonder whether they could have made a better choice, leading to a sense of dissatisfaction.

For instance, after Ritu finally purchased her refrigerator, she couldn't shake the feeling that she might have found a better deal if she had waited a bit longer, or chosen a different model. Despite the fact that the refrigerator was perfectly functional and met all her needs, the lingering regret prevented her from fully enjoying the product.

The constant exposure to new options compounds this dissatisfaction. Consumers are constantly reminded of the existence of better options as new models, designs, and features are released. This creates a cycle of **chronic dissatisfaction**, where the pursuit of the "perfect" product leads to more stress, regret, and anxiety rather than happiness.

Decision Fatigue and Its Effects on Well-Being

Another consequence of too much choice is **decision fatigue**, which occurs when the mental effort required to make decisions becomes exhausting. This fatigue leads to **poor decision-making** and increased stress, as people become overwhelmed by the constant need to evaluate, compare, and choose.

For middle-class families juggling financial responsibilities, work pressures, and personal commitments, the mental energy required to navigate consumer choices can take a toll on their overall well-being. The effects of decision fatigue extend beyond shopping, impacting work effectiveness, patience with family, and increasing the likelihood of making impulsive or regretted decisions.

Simplifying the Decision-Making Process

While the paradox of choice is a reality in today's consumer world, there are ways to **simplify the decision-making process** and reduce the stress that comes with too many options. Here are a few strategies that working-class consumers can use to make more satisfying choices:

1. **Set Clear Priorities:** Before making any purchase, identify what features or aspects are most important to you. For example, if you're buying a smartphone, decide in advance whether battery life, camera quality, or price matters most. By narrowing your focus, you can eliminate options that don't meet your key criteria, making the decision process easier.
2. **Limit the Number of Choices:** Research shows that people are more satisfied when they have fewer options to choose from.

Try to limit your choices to a handful of products or brands that meet your needs, rather than getting bogged down by dozens of alternatives. This reduces the mental effort required to make a decision and leads to greater satisfaction.

3. **Stick to a Budget:** Setting a clear budget helps narrow down your options and prevents you from being tempted by products outside your price range. By focusing only on items within your budget, you can reduce the complexity of your decision and feel more confident of your choices.

4. **Avoid Perfectionism:** Recognize that there is no such thing as the "perfect" choice. Instead of trying to find the best possible option, focus on finding something that meets your needs and brings value to your life. Let go of the idea that there's always a better option out there.

5. **Take Breaks:** If you find yourself overwhelmed by too many options, take a break from shopping and come back to the decision with a rational mind. Sometimes stepping away from the process helps reduce stress and allows you to make a more thoughtful decision.

Conclusion: Less Is More

The paradox of choice teaches us that more options don't necessarily lead to more happiness. For middle-class consumers, who are often navigating a wide range of choices with financial constraints in mind, simplifying the decision-making process is key to finding satisfaction. By setting clear priorities, limiting options, and avoiding the trap of perfectionism, consumers can make more intentional and fulfilling choices without the stress and anxiety that come with too many choices.

Ultimately, **less is more** in consumer decision-making. By embracing simplicity and focusing on what truly matters, we can find greater peace of mind and enjoyment in the things we own.

Chapter 22

The Role of Advertising in Shaping Consumer Culture

In the modern world, advertisements are everywhere. Whether you're scrolling through your social media feed, watching a YouTube video, or walking down the street, you're likely to encounter ads promoting luxury and branded goods. These advertisements don't just sell products; they shape how we see ourselves, what we aspire to, and what we believe we need to be happy.

For the working class, advertising plays a powerful role in reinforcing the idea that owning branded goods is a key to success and fulfillment. However, behind these glossy images and catchy slogans, there's a carefully constructed strategy designed to tap into our emotions, desires, and insecurities.

In this chapter, we will explore how advertising influences consumer behavior, particularly in branded goods. We'll examine the tactics brands use to manipulate our desires and how advertising has helped shape the consumer culture of the middle class in India.

The Evolution of Advertising in India

Advertising in India has evolved significantly over the past few decades, from simple print ads in newspapers to the sophisticated digital marketing strategies we see today. In the early years, advertising was primarily about promoting products and services in local markets. But as India's economy opened up in the 1990s, the landscape changed dramatically.

With the influx of global brands, advertising became a crucial tool for businesses to establish their presence in the Indian market. Companies began using advertisements to not just sell products, but to create **aspirational value** on them. Suddenly, owning a foreign brand or luxury item wasn't just about practicality — it was about showing the world that you had made it.

For the middle class, this shift in advertising had a profound effect. The imagery and messaging used in these ads positioned branded goods as **status symbols**, and the desire to own them became a reflection of one's social standing. As India's economy grew and the middle class expanded, advertising became even more targeted, offering products that promised to fulfill the dreams of upward mobility.

How Advertising Creates Desire

At its core, advertising is about creating **desire**. It's not enough for brands to present their products; they need to make consumers want them, even if they don't actually need them. This is done by tapping into emotional triggers such as happiness, confidence, and success.

For instance, think about a typical luxury car advertisement. You rarely see the car's technical specifications or practical features being emphasized. Instead, the ad shows the car speeding down a scenic road, with an attractive and successful driver behind the wheel. The focus is on the **lifestyle** the car represents, not just the vehicle itself. The message is simple: owning this car will make you feel powerful, successful, and admired.

This is where advertising becomes more than just a way to inform consumers — it becomes a tool for shaping **cultural values**. For the Indian middle class, who are striving to achieve upward mobility, these messages tap into their aspirations. They don't just want to own a product; they want to be part of the lifestyle that the product represents.

Tapping into Aspirations: The Power of Celebrity Endorsements

One of the most effective advertising tactics used in India is **celebrity endorsements**. Bollywood stars, cricketers, and social media influencers are often seen promoting luxury and branded goods, lending their fame and status to these products. For the average consumer, seeing their favorite celebrity associated with a brand creates a powerful desire to own that product.

For example, when a Bollywood star like Shah Rukh Khan endorses a luxury watch, it's not just about the watch itself. It's about the idea that by wearing that watch, you get connected to his success, fame, and glamor. This creates a **halo effect**, where the product becomes more desirable simply because it is associated with someone admired and respected.

Celebrity endorsements also play into the **aspirational mindset** of the middle class. People see their favorite actors or athletes living a luxurious lifestyle, and they want to emulate that. By buying the same brands, they feel a sense of connection to that world, even if only on a symbolic level. This form of advertising reinforces the belief that branded goods are essential for achieving social status and success.

Digital Advertising: The Rise of Influencers

With the rise of social media, a new form of advertising has taken over — **influencer marketing**. Influencers, who are individuals with large followings on platforms like Instagram, YouTube, and Twitter, often promote branded goods to their audiences for sponsorship deals.

For working-class consumers in India, influencers represent a more **relatable** form of advertising. Unlike traditional celebrities, influencers often share their personal lives and experiences, making them seem more approachable. When an influencer promotes a branded product, their followers feel as though they are getting a recommendation from a friend rather than being targeted by a corporate advertisement.

Influencers use platforms like Instagram to showcase luxury goods in a way that feels **authentic** and **personal**. Whether it's a beauty influencer reviewing a designer handbag or a tech influencer showcasing the latest smartphone, these endorsements feel less scripted than traditional ads. This authenticity makes consumers more likely to trust the influencer's opinion and, as a result, more likely to purchase the product.

For working-class consumers, this form of advertising can create an intense **desire for ownership**. Influencers often portray branded goods as accessible luxuries — items that anyone can own with the right mindset, hard work, or a bit of indulgence. This blurs the line between need and want, making it easier for people to justify purchasing branded goods even if they don't need them.

Targeting the Middle Class: Customizing Messages for Aspirational Consumers

One of the key developments in modern advertising is the ability to **target specific audiences** with customized messages. Brands now have access to detailed data about consumers' preferences, behaviors, and interests, allowing them to create personalized ads that address to the desires of different demographic groups.

For the Indian middle class, this means being bombarded with ads that are tailored to their **aspirational desires**. Brands know that working-class consumers want to feel successful, sophisticated, and modern, so they craft advertisements that highlight these values. Whether it's a luxury fashion brand promoting its products as "affordable elegance" or a high-end tech company positioning its products as "the smart choice for ambitious professionals," these ads are designed to make the middle class feel like they are part of an elite group.

This customization creates a sense of **belonging**. The idea of owning a product that has been positioned as a luxury item, but is still within reach, is incredibly appealing to the working-class. It makes them feel that they are moving closer to the lifestyle they aspire to, even if they have to stretch their finances to make it happen.

The Dark Side of Advertising: Creating Insecurities

While advertising can inspire and excite consumers, it can also have a **darker side**. Many ads rely on creating **insecurities** to drive purchases. They subtly imply that if you don't own certain products, you are less successful, less attractive, or less worthy.

For example, beauty and fashion brands often use models with unrealistic body types, flawless skin, and expensive clothing to create a sense of inadequacy in the viewer. The message not only conveys that the product will enhance your life — but that without the product, you won't be good enough.

This is particularly dangerous for working-class consumers, who may already feel pressured to keep up with societal expectations. When advertisements exploit these insecurities, it can lead to **impulse buying**, debt, and a constant feeling of dissatisfaction, as consumers chase after products that promise to fix their insecurities but rarely do.

Breaking Free from Advertising Influence

The first step to breaking free from the influence of advertising is to become aware of the **tactics** being used. By recognizing that ads are designed to create emotional responses and tap into insecurities, consumers can take a more critical approach to their purchasing decisions.

Here are a few strategies to help resist the pressure of advertising:

1. **Be Mindful of Emotional Triggers**: Before making a purchase, ask yourself if the product is something you truly need or if you are being influenced by the emotional appeal of the advertisement.
2. **Limit Exposure to Advertising**: Consider cutting back on the time you spend on social media or consuming content filled with

advertisements. This can help reduce the constant barrage of messages telling you to buy more.

3. **Question the Message**: When you see an advertisement, ask yourself if the message is authentic or if it's designed to create false desires. Being critical of the ad's intent can help you resist its influence.

Conclusion: Advertising's Powerful Grip on Consumer Culture

Advertising has become one of the most powerful forces shaping consumer culture, particularly for branded goods. For the working class, who are constantly bombarded with messages about success, status, and luxury, advertising plays a pivotal role in influencing buying decisions.

While advertisements can inspire, they can also manipulate emotions and create false desires. By understanding how advertising works and taking a more mindful approach to consumption, working-class consumers can begin to resist the pressures of consumerism and make purchasing decisions that align with their genuine needs and values.

Chapter 23

The Rise of Sustainable and Ethical Brands – A New Kind of Luxury

In recent years, a growing number of consumers have become more conscious of the environmental and social impact of their purchasing decisions. This shift has given rise to **sustainable and ethical brands,**

which prioritize eco-friendly materials, fair labor practices, and responsible sourcing. While these brands often come with a premium price tag, they represent a new kind of luxury — one that is rooted in values rather than just aesthetics or status.

For working-class consumers in India, the rise of sustainable luxury offers an alternative to traditional branded goods. Instead of chasing after status symbols, many are beginning to see the appeal of investing in products that align with their values, supporting ethical practices and reducing their carbon footprint. But this shift towards sustainability also raises questions about accessibility, affordability, and whether these products are truly worth the premium.

In this chapter, we'll explore the rise of sustainable and ethical brands, how they are changing the luxury market, and what this trend means for the middle class.

What Is Sustainable Luxury?

Sustainable luxury refers to products that are made with environmentally friendly materials, ethical labor practices, and a commitment to reducing waste and pollution. These brands often focus on the **long-term impact** of their products, aiming to minimize their carbon footprint and promote social responsibility.

Luxury brands like **Stella McCartney, Patagonia,** and **Tata CLiQ Luxury's sustainable collections** have positioned themselves as leaders in this space. They produce high-end goods made from sustainable materials like organic cotton, recycled fabrics, and ethically sourced leather. These products are designed to last longer, reducing the need for constant replacements and lowering overall consumption.

For working-class consumers who are increasingly aware of environmental issues, sustainable luxury represents a way to indulge in high-quality products while also feeling good about their choices.

However, these products often come with a high price tag, raising the question can sustainability can truly be accessible to everyone?

The Ethical Appeal: Fair Trade and Labor Practices

Besides environmental concerns, **ethical labor practices** are a key component of sustainable luxury. Many traditional luxury brands have faced criticism for relying on exploitative labor practices, especially in developing countries. In response, ethical brands have made it a priority to ensure that their products are made by workers who are paid fair wages and work in safe conditions.

The Fair-Trade certification, for example, assures consumers that the products they buy are made ethically. This certification ensures that the people who produce the goods — from farmers to factory workers — are treated fairly and compensated appropriately for their work. Ethical brands also prioritize transparency, often sharing information about their supply chains and the factories where their products are made.

This focus on ethical production resonates with middle-class consumers who want to make more responsible purchasing decisions. While these products may be more expensive, the knowledge that they are supporting fair labor practices can provide a sense of **moral satisfaction** that goes beyond the usual appeal of luxury goods.

Sustainability as a Status Symbol

In the past, luxury goods were often associated with **conspicuous consumption** — the idea that people buy expensive items to show off their wealth and status. However, the rise of sustainable luxury has introduced a new type of status symbol. For many consumers, especially in the middle class, owning eco-friendly or ethically produced products has become a way to signal **social consciousness** and **progressive values.**

For example, wearing a handbag made from recycled materials or buying clothes from a brand that donates a portion of its profits to environmental causes can make a powerful statement. These items represent more than just personal style — they represent a commitment to making the world a better place. In this way, sustainable luxury has become a **badge of honor** for those who want to align their consumption with their values.

This trend is appealing to younger middle-class consumers, who are often more concerned about environmental and social issues. For them, owning sustainable luxury goods is not just about owning something expensive; it's about making a **statement** that they care about the planet and the people who produce their products.

Challenges of Sustainable Luxury for the Middle Class

While sustainable and ethical brands offer many benefits, they also come with challenges, particularly for middle-class consumers. One of the biggest barriers to adopting sustainable luxury is the **cost**. These products are often priced at a rate higher than the traditional luxury goods because they require more expensive materials, fair wages for workers, and sustainable production processes.

For the working-class, this can create a dilemma. On one hand, they may want to support sustainable practices and make more responsible choices. On the other hand, the higher price points of these products may make them feel out of reach, especially for families who are already balancing budgets and trying to save for the future.

To address this issue, some brands have started offering **more affordable options,** or they provide **flexible payment plans** such as **EMI** options to make their products more accessible to a broader audience. However, the question remains: Can sustainability truly be scaled to a level where it's accessible to all, or will it remain a niche market for those who can afford it?

The Role of Technology in Sustainable Luxury

Technology has played a significant role in the rise of sustainable luxury, particularly in how these brands source materials and manufacture their products. Innovations like **recycled fabrics, biodegradable packaging**, and **eco-friendly dyes** have allowed brands to reduce their environmental impact while still producing high-quality goods.

For example, brands like **Patagonia** and **Allbirds** use materials like recycled plastic bottles and natural wool to create durable, eco-friendly clothing and shoes. These materials not only reduce waste but also offer consumers a sustainable alternative to traditional products.

Additionally, technology has made it easier for brands to **track their supply chains** and ensure that their products are made ethically. Blockchain technology, for instance, allows consumers to trace the origins of a product and verify that it was made using fair labor practices and sustainable materials. This transparency is crucial for middle-class consumers who want to make informed decisions about the products they buy.

How Indian Brands Are Embracing Sustainability

The sustainable luxury movement is not just a Western trend. Indian brands are also embracing sustainability and ethical practices, catering to a growing number of middle-class consumers who are concerned about environmental and social issues. Brands like **Nicobar, Anokhi,** and **Amrapali** have built their reputations on producing eco-friendly and ethically sourced products that celebrate India's rich heritage of craftsmanship.

Nicobar, for example, focuses on using natural fabrics like organic cotton and bamboo, while also promoting traditional Indian craftsmanship. **Anokhi** is known for its block-printed textiles, made by artisans using eco-friendly dyes and fair labor practices. These brands not only provide sustainable options but also connect consumers to India's cultural legacy.

For the middle class, these Indian brands offer a way to support both sustainability and **local craftsmanship**, providing an alternative to Western luxury brands. By investing in these products, consumers can feel that they are supporting their country's artisans while also making more ethical choices.

The Future of Sustainable Luxury: Trends to Watch

As the demand for sustainable and ethical products continues to grow, we can expect to see several trends shaping the future of luxury:

1. **Circular Fashion:** The concept of circular fashion, where products are designed to be reused, recycled, or repurposed, is gaining traction. More luxury brands have started to offer **repair services** or **take-back programs**, where consumers can return old products to be recycled or upcycled into new items.
2. **Secondhand Luxury:** The resale market for luxury goods is booming, with platforms like **The RealReal** and **Vestiaire Collective** offering consumers the chance to buy pre-owned luxury items at a lower price. This trend is appealing to working-class consumers who want to own luxury goods while also making sustainable choices.
3. **Eco-Friendly Materials:** We can expect to see more brands experimenting with innovative materials, such as **vegan leather, biodegradable fabrics**, and **3D-printed materials**. These materials not only reduce environmental impact but also provide

a unique selling point for brands that want to stand out in the luxury market.

4. **Transparency and Accountability**: As consumers demand more transparency, brands will need to be more forthcoming about their supply chains, labor practices, and environmental impact. This will probably lead to more **certifications** and **eco-labels** that allow consumers to make informed decisions about the products they buy.

Conclusion: A New Era of Responsible Luxury

The rise of sustainable and ethical luxury represents a shift in how we think about consumption. No longer is luxury solely about status and exclusivity; it's also about **responsibility** and **values**. For middle-class consumers in India and around the world, sustainable luxury offers an opportunity to align their purchasing decisions with their beliefs, supporting products that are better for the planet and the people who make them.

However, this shift also presents challenges, particularly in terms of affordability and accessibility. As the sustainable luxury market grows, it will be essential for brands to find ways to make these products more accessible to a broader audience without compromising on their values.

In the end, sustainable luxury is about more than just owning beautiful products. It's about creating a better future for everyone — one where quality, responsibility, and ethics come together to redefine what it means to live luxuriously.

Chapter 24

Real Stories of Breaking Free – Case Studies of Conscious Consumers

In a world where brands and status symbols seem to define success, it's refreshing to see people who have consciously chosen a different path. These individuals have discovered that true fulfillment lies in experiences, relationships, and purpose—not in logos or luxury. The following real-life stories offer a glimpse into the journeys of people who stepped away from brand-driven consumerism and found joy in simplicity. Their experiences are a testament to the power of intentional living and can serve as an inspiration for anyone looking for value beyond the brand.

Case Study 1: Nisha's Journey to Financial Freedom

Nisha, a successful marketing executive in her 30s, once prided herself on her collection of luxury handbags and accessories. Every month, she'd allocate a chunk of her salary to designer pieces, each new item adding a sense of accomplishment and status. But as her collection grew, so did her financial anxiety. She began to feel trapped in a cycle of overspending and wondered if these items were bringing her the satisfaction she was seeking.

A turning point came after a candid conversation with a close friend who practiced minimalism. Nisha decided to take a "brand detox" for a month, avoiding luxury stores and unsubscribing from promotional newsletters. As she stepped back from her brand-driven habits, she noticed something profound: her stress levels dropped, and her savings grew. With the extra money, she could plan a solo trip she'd been dreaming of for years.

Reflecting on her journey, Nisha shares, "I found freedom when I started investing in experiences rather than things." Today, she enjoys a sense of financial security and fulfillment that no handbag ever brought her. Her story reminds us that sometimes, the most valuable luxury is financial peace.

Case Study 2: Ramesh and Priya's Shift to Conscious Living

Ramesh and Priya, a couple in their early 40s, were known among friends for their collection of high-end home decor and electronics. Over time, however, their beautifully decorated house started to feel more like a display showroom than a home. Their possessions, while aesthetically pleasing, felt like empty symbols of success.

After watching a documentary on sustainable living, the couple decided to make a change. They donated items they rarely used, moved into a cozier home, and began focusing their time and money on travel and quality family moments. "Our home is simpler now, but it feels more like us," Ramesh reflects. They found joy in decluttering and rediscovered their passion for exploring new places together. Priya adds, "It's funny how letting go of things made us feel so much richer."

Their journey to conscious living shows that sometimes, the most valuable possessions are intangible: connection, shared experiences, and a genuine sense of belonging.

Case Study 3: Anil's Minimalist Makeover

Anil, a software developer in his 20s, once saw branded clothing as essential for projecting a "successful" image. Each month, he'd invest in new designer wear, convinced it was crucial for his self-confidence and career. But with each purchase, he found himself longing for more, never quite satisfied with his current wardrobe.

Curious about minimalism, Anil decided to try a "capsule wardrobe"—a small collection of versatile, high-quality pieces. As he pared down his clothing to simple, functional items, he was surprised to discover that his confidence grew. Without the pressure to keep up with the latest trends, he felt more grounded and self-assured. "I realized that success isn't about what you wear; it's about what you achieve," Anil says.

Anil's minimalist makeover taught him that less can indeed be more, and that his self-worth is defined by his contributions, not his clothes.

Case Study 4: The Gupta Family's Digital Detox

With three teenagers at home, the Gupta family often found themselves swept up in the digital trend of sharing every moment online. Dinners, vacations, and even small weekend outings became photo ops, with each family member focused more on capturing moments than experiencing them.

Realizing that social media was driving their consumption habits, the family decided to try a "digital detox" for one month. During this time, they avoided social media, put a pause on branded purchases, and instead focused on meaningful family activities. They spent evenings cooking together, playing board games, and talking without phones nearby. Over time, they noticed a shift—not only were they spending less, but they were also more connected and content.

Mrs. Gupta reflects, "Our home feels more relaxed, like a real sanctuary rather than a place where we try to impress others." The Gupta family's digital detox helped them see that true happiness often lies in simplicity and togetherness, not in social media likes or luxury items.

Case Study 5: Sita's Discovery of Local Artisans

Sita, an art teacher in her 50s, had long admired luxury handbags but struggled with spending so much on a single item. During a visit to a local artisan market, she discovered beautifully crafted handbags made by local designers. Intrigued by the stories of the artisans, she decided to buy one, finding it more personal and meaningful than a big brand item.

Since then, Sita has sought out other local products, learning to appreciate the craftsmanship and unique touch each item carries. "There's a sense of pride in supporting real people and communities," Sita explains. She now feels that each purchase has a purpose beyond consumption, adding meaning to her belongings.

Sita's journey reminds us that luxury doesn't have to be a brand. Supporting local artisans and finding joy in the artistry behind every item often reveals true value.

Key Takeaways

The stories shared in this chapter highlight a common theme: true fulfillment often lies in simplicity, intention, and authenticity, not in branded goods. Here are some key takeaways:

1. **Redefine Luxury**: For Nisha and others, redefining luxury as experiences, financial freedom, or meaningful connections brought them more joy than any branded item ever could.
2. **Focus on What Matters**: Ramesh and Priya's journey to a simpler life shows that letting go of unnecessary possessions can make space for what truly matters—family, shared experiences, and a genuine sense of home.
3. **Embrace Minimalism**: Anil's decision to try a minimalist wardrobe led him to discover that confidence doesn't come from brand labels; it comes from self-assurance and a focus on personal growth.
4. **Limit Social Media Influence**: The Gupta family's digital detox helped them reconnect and find happiness beyond branded purchases, reminding us that we don't need to broadcast our lives to find meaning.

5. **Support Local Artisans:** Sita's choice to invest in local, handcrafted goods illustrates that value can often be found in the personal connection behind each item, rather than the logo on it.

Final Reflection

As these stories show, breaking free from brand obsession doesn't require giving up quality or style—it's about discovering what truly enriches our lives. Whether it's spending on experiences, embracing minimalism, or supporting local artisans, these choices reflect the freedom and joy that comes from living intentionally.

In a world that often equates value with price, these individuals remind us that the most priceless things—peace, connection, purpose—are often found in the simplest of moments. May their journeys inspire you to seek fulfillment not in brands but in the beauty of an authentic life.

Chapter 25

The Future of Luxury: Emerging Trends and Predictions

The world of luxury is constantly evolving, shaped by changes in technology, social values, and consumer awareness. As more people seek meaningful, sustainable alternatives, the luxury industry has begun to adapt, redefining what it means to live "luxuriously." In this chapter, we'll explore the emerging trends that are reshaping the luxury market and look at how the future of luxury may prioritize sustainability, personalization, and ethical impact over status and materialism.

1. Sustainable Luxury: The Rise of Eco-Conscious Brands

With growing awareness of environmental issues, many consumers are rethinking their purchases and choosing brands that align with sustainable values. This shift is very evident in the luxury market, where eco-friendly practices are becoming a priority. Today's luxury shoppers, especially millennials and Gen Z, are looking for brands that embrace ethical sourcing, eco-friendly materials, and responsible production.

Brands like Stella McCartney, Patagonia, and Veja are leading the way, offering products that are both high quality and environmentally friendly. They use materials like organic cotton, recycled leather, and responsibly sourced wool, proving that luxury doesn't have to come at the expense of the planet. By choosing sustainable brands, consumers are redefining luxury as something that contributes positively to the world.

This trend suggests a future where "green luxury" becomes the norm, and where environmental impact is as crucial as style and status.

2. Virtual and Digital Luxury Experiences

The digital age has brought about a new form of luxury: virtual and digital experiences. With advancements in technology, luxury is no longer limited to physical possessions—it now includes virtual goods, experiences, and even NFTs (non-fungible tokens). Many luxury brands are experimenting with digital assets, allowing consumers to own virtual items that can be displayed in the digital world, such as virtual art, fashion items, or unique digital collectibles.

Luxury brands like Gucci, Balenciaga, and Louis Vuitton are already creating virtual clothing collections and interactive digital experiences. These items offer a new form of exclusivity, appealing to digital-savvy consumers who enjoy the novelty of virtual ownership. With the rise of the "metaverse"—virtual spaces where people can interact in immersive online worlds—digital luxury could become a significant part of the future market.

As technology continues to develop, we can expect luxury brands to expand further into the virtual space, where exclusivity isn't tied to physical products but to experiences that blend the digital and real worlds.

3. Personalization and Customization: The Ultimate Luxury Experience

In a world where mass production is the norm, customization and personalization have become the new luxury. Consumers today want products that feel unique and tailored to their tastes, and luxury brands are increasingly offering personalized experiences to meet this demand. Whether it's a monogrammed handbag, bespoke clothing, or custom fragrances, personalization adds a sense of exclusivity and connection to luxury items.

Brands like Hermès, Rolls-Royce, and Louis Vuitton offer bespoke services, allowing clients to co-create their items, choosing everything from materials to colors and design elements. This trend is transforming the luxury experience from one of passive consumption to active participation, where customers play a role in crafting their possessions.

As personalization becomes more accessible, it's likely that even mid-tier brands will adopt these practices, making customized luxury a standard option rather than an exception.

4. The Shift to Experiential Luxury

While traditional luxury has focused on material goods, there is a growing trend toward experiential luxury—prioritizing experiences over possessions. Consumers, particularly millennials and Gen Z, are increasingly choosing to spend on experiences that create memories rather than physical items. High-end travel, gourmet dining, wellness retreats, and exclusive events are becoming the new markers of luxury, reflecting a shift in values toward personal growth and meaningful experiences.

Companies like Airbnb Luxe, which offers unique, luxurious stays, and brands like Aman Resorts, which provide bespoke wellness experiences, are catering to this demand for experiential luxury. People are seeking out activities that enrich their lives, broaden their perspectives, and foster personal connections, moving away from the emphasis on tangible possessions.

In the future, luxury may come to represent not what one owns, but the life one leads—focusing on fulfillment, learning, and personal exploration.

---

5. Minimalism and Mindful Consumption

The rise of minimalism has had a significant impact on the luxury market, encouraging people to invest in fewer, higher-quality items that add real value to their lives. This trend is driven by a desire for simplicity, mindfulness, and a focus on essentials rather than excess. For many, luxury now means owning less but choosing items that are well-crafted, durable, and aligned with personal values.

Brands like Cuyana and Everlane promote a "fewer, better" philosophy, encouraging consumers to select timeless, versatile pieces that can be worn for years. This minimalist approach to luxury emphasizes quality over quantity, challenging the traditional notion that luxury is about owning many expensive items.

As people continue to embrace minimalism, the future of luxury may prioritize mindful consumption, where people invest in items that truly matter and reflect their values, rather than accumulating for the sake of status.

---

6. The Ethical Consumer: A Shift in Values

Today's consumers are more ethically aware, valuing transparency and responsibility in the brands they support. From fair wages for workers to cruelty-free products, the ethical consumer movement is driving change in the luxury market. Brands are increasingly disclosing their supply chains, committing to fair labor practices, and making strides toward humane and cruelty-free production.

Luxury brands like Tiffany & Co. and Cartier have adopted "responsible sourcing" practices for their diamonds and gemstones, while other brands focus on ethical treatment of animals and environmentally friendly packaging. This shift reflects a broader change in consumer values, where people want to support brands that align with their morals and contribute positively to society.

In the future, the ethical consumer may redefine luxury as not only exclusive but also responsible, holding brands accountable for their impact on people and the planet.

Key Takeaways

As we look to the future, luxury is becoming less about opulence and more about responsibility, personalization, and experience. Here are some key trends shaping the future of luxury:

1. **Sustainable Luxury**: Eco-conscious brands are redefining luxury, with environmental responsibility becoming a key factor in high-end markets.
2. **Virtual Luxury**: Digital assets and virtual experiences are expanding the luxury market into the virtual world, offering alternative forms of exclusivity.
3. **Personalized Experiences**: Customization and bespoke options are making luxury more personal, allowing consumers to co-create their items.
4. **Experiential Luxury**: Experiences are becoming the new currency of luxury, focusing on personal growth and fulfillment over material items.
5. **Minimalism and Mindfulness**: The "fewer, better" approach is redefining luxury as quality over quantity, aligning with a minimalist, intentional lifestyle.
6. **Ethical Consumption**: Consumers are prioritizing brands that uphold ethical standards, pushing the luxury industry toward greater transparency and responsibility.

Final Reflection

The future of luxury is evolving, reflecting shifts in values and priorities. As people become more aware of the impact of their purchases, they are redefining luxury to align with their principles and aspirations. This emerging era of luxury celebrates not just material wealth but a commitment to authenticity, sustainability, and ethical responsibility.

As you navigate your relationship with branded goods, remember that luxury can be more than a display of wealth—it can reflect values, choices, and an intentional approach to life. The most meaningful luxuries often aren't those with a high price tag, but those that enrich our lives in ways that truly matter.

Chapter 26

Minimalism vs. Consumerism – A New Trend for the Middle Class?

As branded goods become more accessible to the middle class, there's also a growing counter-movement: **minimalism**. Minimalism, which encourages people to live with less and focus on what truly matters, challenges the very foundation of consumerism and the desire for luxury goods. In a world where advertisements, influencers, and social pressures constantly encourage buying more, minimalism advocates for cutting back on unnecessary possessions and emphasizing simplicity, mindfulness, and intentionality in everyday life.

For many middle-class Indians, minimalism offers an alternative approach to living — one that rejects the idea that happiness and success are tied to material wealth. But at the same time, the allure of branded goods and consumer culture remains strong, creating a tension between these two ideologies. In this chapter, we'll explore the rise of minimalism and its relevance for the middle class in India, examining how it contrasts with the desire for branded goods and what it means for the future of consumption.

What Is Minimalism?

Minimalism is a lifestyle philosophy that encourages people to live with fewer material possessions, focusing on what brings real value to their lives. Rather than accumulating things, minimalism emphasizes the importance of **experiences, relationships, and personal growth**. It's about stripping away the excess and finding satisfaction in the essentials.

Minimalism can be understood as decluttering one's home, reducing waste, or making more thoughtful purchasing decisions. It also involves a shift in mindset — from seeking validation through material goods to finding contentment in non-material pursuits. The movement is often associated with concepts like **mindfulness, sustainability,** and **financial independence.**

Minimalism has gained popularity around the world, particularly in Western countries, where overconsumption has led to environmental and psychological concerns. However, in India, where the middle class is still growing and many people are just beginning to access luxury goods, the idea of minimalism presents a unique challenge. How do you balance the desire for upward mobility with the idea of living with less?

The Appeal of Minimalism for the Middle Class

For working-class Indians, the appeal of minimalism lies in its promise of **simplicity** and **freedom**. As consumerism takes hold and more branded goods flood the market, many people find themselves overwhelmed by the pressure to keep up with trends and accumulate possessions. Minimalism offers a way to break free from this cycle, focusing instead on what truly matters.

One of the key drivers of minimalism is **financial independence**. For working-class families, the constant pursuit of branded goods can lead to debt, financial stress, and a feeling of never having enough. Minimalism encourages people to prioritize their financial health, save money, and invest in long-term goals rather than short-term desires. This is relevant for the middle class, who are often balancing the need to provide for their families with the pressure to maintain a certain standard of living.

Moreover, minimalism aligns with the growing concern about **sustainability** and the environmental impact of overconsumption. As people become aware of the damage caused by fast fashion, electronic waste, and unsustainable manufacturing practices, minimalism offers a way to reduce one's carbon footprint and make more responsible choices. For middle-class consumers who are increasingly conscious of these issues, minimalism provides a way to align their values with their lifestyle.

Minimalism vs. Consumerism: The Tension Between Two Ideologies

At its core, minimalism is the opposite of **Consumerism**, which encourages people to buy more, own more, and equate success with material wealth. Consumerism thrives on the idea that more is better — that owning the latest gadgets, designer clothes, or luxury cars will bring happiness and social status. Branded goods, particularly luxury items, are often marketed as status symbols that will elevate one's social standing and fulfill personal desires.

For the middle class in India, this creates a **tension**. On one hand, there is the desire to achieve success through material wealth, to own the kinds of branded goods that signal upward mobility and modernity. On the other hand, there is a growing awareness that these possessions do not necessarily lead to lasting happiness or fulfillment. Minimalism challenges the consumerist mindset by arguing that less is more — that true contentment comes not from accumulating things, but from focusing on what is truly important.

This tension is evident in the younger middle class, who are more exposed to global trends, social media, and Western ideas about consumption. Many young professionals in India aspire to own luxury goods, but they are also becoming more aware of the **mental and emotional toll** that constant consumption can take. Minimalism offers a way to opt out of the rat race, encouraging people to find joy in simplicity rather than the endless pursuit of material goods.

Minimalism in the Indian Context

While minimalism is often associated with Western lifestyles, its principles are deeply rooted in Indian philosophy and traditions. Concepts like **simple living** and **non-attachment** have long been part of Indian culture, particularly in spiritual practices like **Buddhism** and

Hinduism. The idea of finding happiness in simplicity, rather than material wealth, is a core tenet of many Indian philosophies.

For example, the **Gandhian philosophy** of living with minimal possessions and focusing on self-reliance has influenced generations in Indian. Mahatma Gandhi himself a strong advocate of simplicity, famously said, "The world has enough for everyone's needs, but not everyone's greed." This message resonates with the principles of modern minimalism, which encourages people to live with less and find contentment in non-material pursuits.

However, in contemporary Indian society, minimalism faces certain challenges. As more people enter the middle class and gain access to luxury goods, the pressure to consume increases. Festivals, weddings, and family celebrations often come with expectations of lavish spending and gift-giving, making it difficult for many to embrace minimalism fully. The cultural significance of material wealth — particularly in terms of status and social validation — remains strong in many parts of the country.

Despite these challenges, a growing number of middle-class Indians are adopting minimalist principles, seeking to simplify their lives and reduce the clutter, both physical and mental. For these individuals, minimalism is not about renouncing luxury entirely, but about making more **intentional** choices and focusing on what truly adds value to their lives.

How Minimalism Challenges Branded Goods

One of the key ways minimalism challenges the dominance of branded goods is by encouraging consumers to **question the value** of their purchases. Minimalism encourages people to ask themselves whether they truly need something before buying it, which promotes mindful consumption. This sharply contrasts with the impulse-driven nature of consumerism, where marketers often encourage people to buy things based on emotion, social pressure, or advertising.

For working-class consumers who are constantly bombarded with messages about the importance of owning branded goods, minimalism offers a way to push back against these pressures. Instead of feeling the need to keep up with trends or impress others with luxury items, minimalism encourages people to focus on what brings them joy and fulfillment on a deeper level.

In many ways, minimalism is about **redefining success**. While consumerism equates success with material wealth, minimalism argues that success can be found in experiences, relationships, and personal growth. This shift in perspective challenges the traditional narrative of luxury and branded goods as the ultimate markers of achievement.

The Impact of Social Media on Minimalism and Consumerism

Social media plays a crucial role in shaping both minimalism and consumerism. While platforms like Instagram and Facebook are filled with influencers showcasing luxury brands and promoting consumerist ideals. The constant exposure to curated images of wealth, beauty, and success creates a sense of **FOMO (fear of missing out)**, driving many people to buy more and consume more in order to keep up.

Social media has also become a platform for **minimalism advocates**, who share their experiences of living with less and encourage others to embrace simplicity. Influencers who promote minimalism often share tips on decluttering, living mindfully, and making more intentional choices. These voices provide an alternative to the consumerist messages that dominate social media, offering a different perspective on what it means to live a fulfilling life.

For the middle class in India, social media can be both a source of inspiration and a source of pressure. While many seek simpler lives, they are constantly bombarded with images of luxury and success, making it hard to resist consumerism. The challenge lies in navigating these competing messages and finding a balance between enjoying material goods and living with intention.

Minimalism and Financial Freedom

One of the most significant benefits of minimalism for middle-class consumers is the potential for **financial freedom**. By focusing on what truly matters and cutting back on unnecessary spending, minimalism allows people to save more, invest in long-term goals, and reduce debt. This is relevant for working-class families who may feel the financial strain of keeping up with consumerist pressures.

Minimalism encourages people to rethink their spending habits and prioritize **financial security** over short-term gratification. Instead of spending money on luxury goods that may bring temporary satisfaction, minimalism advocates for investing in experiences, personal growth, and long-term financial stability. For many, this shift in mindset can lead to a greater sense of peace and fulfillment, as they are no longer tied to the endless cycle of consumption.

Conclusion: Finding a Balance Between Minimalism and Consumerism

Minimalism and consumerism represent two opposing forces in the modern world, and for middle-class Indians, navigating these ideologies can be challenging. On one hand, the desire for upward mobility, success, and branded goods remains strong. On the other hand, there is a growing awareness that material possessions alone do not bring lasting happiness.

For many, the solution lies in finding a **balance** between these two approaches. Rather than fully embracing one ideology or the other, middle-class consumers can adopt elements of minimalism while still enjoying the occasional luxury purchase. By focusing on intentionality and mindful consumption, they can avoid the pitfalls of consumerism while still appreciating the beauty and craftsmanship of branded goods.

In the end, minimalism offers a way to reclaim control over one's life, encouraging people to prioritize what truly matters — whether that's family, experiences, or personal growth. By rejecting the idea that success is measured by material wealth, middle-class Indians can find a new path forward, one that aligns with both their values and their aspirations.

Chapter 27

A Practical Guide to Conscious Consumption

As we've explored throughout this book, the allure of branded goods and luxury items is powerful—but it's not always fulfilling. Many of us get caught up in the excitement of owning designer labels, often without realizing the impact this lifestyle can have on our financial well-being and mental peace. This chapter serves as a practical guide to help you make more conscious choices. By focusing on mindful consumption, you can take control of your spending, prioritize what truly matters, and find greater satisfaction beyond the brand.

---

1. Identifying Needs vs. Wants

The first step to conscious consumption is learning to differentiate between needs and wants. While it's natural to desire luxury items, understanding whether they truly add value to your life can help prevent impulsive purchases. Here are a few questions to consider:

- **Why do I want this item?** Are you drawn to the brand, the quality, or the status it brings?
- **Will this purchase improve my life meaningfully?** If not, it might be more of a want than a need.
- **Can I afford it comfortably?** If buying this item stretches your budget or adds financial stress, it may not be worth it.

By taking a moment to reflect on these questions, you can gain clarity on your motivations and make more thoughtful choices.

---

2. Setting Financial Priorities

Creating a budget that reflects your values and goals is essential for conscious consumption. When you prioritize your spending, you'll find it easier to resist the pull of luxury items that don't align with your needs. Here's a simple strategy to get started:

- **Define Your Financial Goals:** Whether it's saving for a home, paying off debt, or traveling, identifying your priorities can help you stay focused.

- **Allocate Spending Categories**: Assign a budget to different categories, such as essentials, experiences, and discretionary spending. This will help you see how much you can comfortably spend on luxury without compromising other areas.
- **Evaluate Purchases Regularly**: Periodically review your purchases and spending patterns. Ask yourself if they reflect your goals or if there's room to adjust.

This approach to budgeting empowers you to enjoy luxuries without feeling pressured to constantly "keep up" with brand-driven trends.

---

3. Embracing the "Branded Goods Detox"

If you're struggling to break free from the cycle of branded purchases, consider a short "branded goods detox." This exercise involves temporarily avoiding the purchase of luxury or branded items, giving yourself the space to reassess your values and spending habits. Here's how it works:

- **Set a Timeframe**: Start with a month-long detox where you consciously avoid buying any branded or luxury items.
- **Replace the Habit**: During this period, focus on experiences, self-care, or creative hobbies that don't involve shopping.
- **Reflect on Your Feelings**: Notice how you feel throughout the detox. Do you miss the luxury items, or do you feel relieved by the reduced pressure to consume?

Many people find that a detox helps them break impulsive habits and feel more at peace with their spending. It's a great way to reset and reflect on what truly brings happiness.

---

4. Questions to Ask Before a Purchase

To avoid impulsive spending, especially on luxury items, try asking yourself these questions before making a purchase:

- **Do I already have something similar?** Often, we buy items we don't need simply because they're trendy or on sale.
- **Will this item bring long-term value?** Think about whether the item will still be useful a year from now.
- **Is this purchase aligned with my values?** If your goal is to prioritize savings or reduce consumption, consider if this purchase supports those goals.

These questions can serve as a checklist, helping you evaluate each purchase thoughtfully and mindfully.

---

5. Practicing Gratitude and Contentment

One of the most powerful tools for conscious consumption is cultivating gratitude. When we focus on what we already have, we're less likely to feel the need to buy more. Practicing gratitude can shift your mindset from "I need this to be happy" to "I already have enough." Here's how you can integrate gratitude into your daily life:

- **Keep a Gratitude Journal**: Every day, write a few things you're grateful for, whether it's relationships, experiences, or simple joys.
- **Reflect on Non-Material Values**: Think about the things that make you feel truly fulfilled—these are often experiences, connections, or personal achievements, not material items.
- **Celebrate Your Choices**: Recognize and appreciate the choices you've made toward mindful consumption. Celebrating small wins can keep you motivated to live intentionally.

Gratitude helps reduce the desire for excess, allowing you to find joy in simplicity and authenticity.

---

6. Supporting Local and Sustainable Brands

If you choose to buy branded items, consider supporting local artisans or sustainable brands that align with your values. These purchases not only offer quality but also contribute to a positive impact on the environment and community. Here's how to make conscious choices:

- **Research Sustainable Brands**: Look for brands that prioritize ethical practices, fair labor, and eco-friendly materials.
- **Support Local Artisans**: Buying from local creators allows you to enjoy unique, handmade items that often have a story behind them.
- **Quality Over Quantity**: Instead of buying many items, consider investing in fewer, high-quality pieces that are timeless and long-lasting.

By choosing sustainable and local brands, you can enjoy the luxury of quality goods while supporting responsible practices.

---

7. Embracing a Minimalist Mindset

Minimalism isn't about living with nothing; it's about living with what truly matters. By embracing a minimalist mindset, you can shift your focus from accumulating possessions to cultivating experiences and personal growth. Here's how to get started:

- **Declutter Your Space**: Start by removing items you no longer use or need. A clean, organized space often leads to a clearer mind.
- **Invest in experiences**: Rather than spending on material goods, try spending on experiences that create lasting memories, such as travel, learning, or hobbies.
- **Focus on quality**: When you do make a purchase, choose quality over quantity. Minimalism encourages thoughtful ownership, where each item adds real value.

Adopting a minimalist approach to life can free you from the cycle of constant consumption, bringing you closer to a sense of contentment and peace.

Key Takeaways

Conscious consumption is about making choices that align with your values, goals, and well-being. Here's a quick recap of how you can integrate mindful habits into your life:

1. **Differentiate Needs from Wants**: Understanding the difference can help you avoid impulsive purchases and focus on what truly adds value.
2. **Set Financial Priorities**: Creating a budget that reflects your values empowers you to enjoy luxuries without compromising your goals.
3. **Try a Branded Goods Detox**: A temporary break from branded items can help reset your mindset and reduce reliance on luxury.
4. **Ask Intentional Questions**: Simple questions before each purchase can prevent impulse buying and encourage thoughtful consumption.
5. **Cultivate Gratitude**: Focusing on what you have can reduce the urge to acquire more and bring lasting happiness.
6. **Support Sustainable and Local Brands**: Ethical brands allow you to enjoy luxury with a positive impact on the environment and community.
7. **Embrace Minimalism**: Shifting focus from things to experiences fosters a simpler, more intentional life.

Final Reflection

True fulfillment doesn't come from the brands we wear or the items we own—it comes from aligning our lives with our values and priorities.

By practicing conscious consumption, we can break free from the endless cycle of acquiring more and discover a sense of peace, purpose, and satisfaction. Luxury isn't just about the price tag; it's about living authentically and choosing what truly enriches our lives.

As you continue on this journey, remember that the value of your life isn't defined by the logos you display but by the joy, purpose, and connections you cultivate. Here's to embracing a life that is rich in meaning, not in materialism.

End of Part VI: Breaking Free and Finding Real Value

Part VI offered practical strategies for moving beyond the cycle of luxury-driven consumerism and discovering fulfillment in simplicity, experiences, and personal growth. Key takeaways from this part include:

1. **Redefining Success**: True success often comes from personal growth, relationships, and experiences, rather than material possessions.

2. **Embracing Minimalism**: Minimalism encourages mindful consumption, focusing on quality over quantity and leading to a more meaningful life with less financial and mental burden.

3. **Finding True Wealth**: The most valuable aspects of life, such as health, happiness, and genuine connections, are priceless and can't be bought.

4. **Mindful Consumption**: Learning to differentiate between needs and wants, setting financial priorities, and practicing gratitude are essential steps toward a more fulfilling life.

5. **Adopting a Personalized Definition of Luxury**: Luxury doesn't have to mean expensive—it can mean anything that adds value to your life, whether it's time, freedom, or peace of mind.

Conclusion: Striking a Balance – Navigating the World of Branded Goods

In a world that constantly bombards us with advertisements, social pressures, and the allure of luxury, it's easy to feel caught in the endless pursuit of branded goods. For the Indian middle class, this desire is further fueled by aspirations of upward mobility, cultural expectations, and the promise of success through material wealth. Branded goods have become symbols of status, achievement, and belonging, but they also come with their share of financial strain, emotional exhaustion, and even dissatisfaction.

Throughout this book, we've explored the many facets of branded goods and luxury, from the psychological manipulation of advertisements to the social pressure to keep up with trends. We've looked at how consumerism manifests in India's growing middle class, and how branded goods are often seen as markers of success, both in personal and social spheres. Yet, we've also seen the rise of counter-movements like minimalism, which challenge the idea that happiness and fulfillment come from material wealth.

The **truth** is that there is no one-size-fits-all answer. For some, branded goods offer a sense of pride, confidence, and achievement, while for others, they may lead to financial strain and a never-ending desire for more. The key to navigating this world lies in **balance**. It's about understanding the true value of what we buy, making mindful decisions, and aligning our purchases with our long-term goals and personal values.

The Middle-Class Dilemma: Want vs. Need

One of the core challenges for the middle class is distinguishing between **wants** and **needs**. Branded goods are often positioned as needs — as essentials for fitting in, gaining social approval, or proving success. However, as we've discussed, many of these goods fulfill **emotional desires** rather than practical necessities. By understanding the psychological and cultural forces at play, middle-class consumers can make more informed decisions about whether a branded item truly adds value to their lives.

Mindful Consumption: A New Approach to Luxury

Rather than rejecting luxury entirely or falling into the trap of consumerism, the solution lies in adopting a mindset of **mindful consumption**. This means being intentional about what we buy, focusing on quality over quantity, and ensuring that our purchases align with our personal goals and values. For example, investing in a high-quality branded product that will last for years can be more rewarding than buying multiple cheaper items that quickly wear out.

Mindful consumption also involves considering the **ethical** and **environmental** implications of our purchases. As more consumers become aware of the impact of fast fashion, unsustainable production practices, and exploitative labor, there is a growing demand for **sustainable and ethical brands**. Supporting these brands allows consumers to enjoy luxury while making responsible choices that reflect their values.

The Future of Branded Goods: A More Conscious Consumer

As India's middle class continues to grow and evolve, the relationship with branded goods will probably become more nuanced. While the allure of luxury will always exist, there is also a rising awareness of the need for **financial independence, environmental sustainability**, and **ethical consumption**. This shift towards more conscious consumption reflects a broader global trend, where consumers are demanding more from the brands they support.

For the middle class, the challenge will be to navigate this changing landscape, balancing the desire for luxury with the need for financial stability and personal fulfillment. By adopting a more mindful approach to branded goods, middle-class consumers can enjoy the benefits of luxury without falling into the trap of overconsumption or debt.

Final Thoughts: Defining Success on Your Own Terms

Ultimately, the pursuit of branded goods is about more than just material possessions — it's about how we define success, happiness, and fulfillment. For some, success may be owning a luxury car or a designer outfit; for others, it may be achieving financial independence, building meaningful relationships, or pursuing personal growth.

The key is to **define success on your own terms**, rather than being swayed by societal pressures or advertisements that tell you what you should want. By focusing on what truly matters to you, whether it's branded goods or experiences, you can create a life that brings genuine happiness and satisfaction.

Branded goods can be a source of joy, pride, and even financial investment when approached mindfully. But they are not the only path to success. As you navigate the complexities of modern consumer culture, remember that true fulfillment comes from within — not from the labels on the products you own, but from the values you uphold and the life you choose to lead.

Discussion Questions and Reflection Prompts

As you conclude this journey through *The Illusion of Luxury: Living Beyond Labels and Logos*, consider taking a few moments to reflect on the themes and ideas presented. These questions and prompts are designed to help you deepen your understanding of your own consumer habits, explore your values, and consider meaningful changes in how you relate to luxury and branded goods. Use these questions for personal reflection, journal entries, or even discussions with friends and family.

---

1. Understanding Your Own Motivations

- **Why do I feel drawn to branded items?** Think about what appeals to you most about luxury goods. Is it the quality, the status, or something else?
- **Do I feel that luxury items reflect who I am?** Reflect on whether branded goods genuinely represent your personality or if they serve more than a way to meet external expectations.
- **What would my life look like if I focused less on material possessions?** Visualize a lifestyle where your sense of self-worth isn't tied to luxury. How would it affect your choices, relationships, and happiness?

---

2. Examining Social Pressures and Influences

- **How has social media influenced my spending habits?** Reflect on whether seeing luxury items on social platforms has led to any impulse buys or feelings of inadequacy.

- **Do I compare myself to others based on what they own?** Think about how often you find yourself comparing your life to others based on their possessions. How does this comparison make you feel?
- **In what ways have friends or family influenced my view of success and luxury?** Consider whether your views on luxury are shaped by the people close to you and how their opinions affect your purchasing decisions.

---

3. Redefining Success and Happiness

- **What truly makes me feel successful?** Reflect on what gives you a genuine sense of accomplishment. Is it material wealth, personal growth, meaningful relationships, or something else?
- **When do I feel the happiest?** Think about the moments in your life when you've felt the most content and fulfilled. Were these moments tied to luxury items or experiences?
- **How can I focus more on experiences rather than possessions?** Explore ways to prioritize experiences that enrich your life, such as travel, learning, or quality time with loved ones, over accumulating things.

---

4. Practical Steps Toward Conscious Consumption

- **What is one area where I can reduce spending on luxury?** Identify a specific area, such as clothing or technology, where you can cut back on branded purchases and focus on simpler, more intentional choices.
- **How can I practice minimalism?** Consider small steps you can take, like decluttering your home or buying only what you truly need, to shift your focus from quantity to quality.

- **What values do I want my spending to reflect?** Reflect on your core values—whether it's sustainability, quality, or supporting local artisans—and think about how you can make purchases that align with them.

5. Exploring Gratitude and Contentment

- **What am I grateful for that isn't tied to luxury or brands?** Write the people, experiences, and aspects of your life that bring you joy without a price tag attached.
- **How can I cultivate contentment with what I already have?** Reflect on ways to appreciate your current possessions and life circumstances without the constant need for new, branded items.
- **What steps can I take to reduce the influence of FOMO (fear of missing out)?** Consider how you might limit exposure to advertisements or social media triggers that make you feel you're missing out on luxury experiences.

6. Reflecting on Minimalism and Long-Term Goals

- **What are my long-term financial and personal goals?** Write the goals you have for the next five or ten years and consider how luxury purchases fit—or don't fit—into those plans.
- **How would I define "enough" in terms of possessions?** Reflect on what a comfortable, fulfilling life would look like if consumer culture did not influence it. What do you truly need to feel content?
- **What does luxury mean to me personally?** Define what luxury means to you, separate from societal expectations or brand influence. Is it quality, comfort, freedom, or something else?

Final Reflection

These prompts invite you to consider what role luxury items should play in your life. By examining your values, motivations, and the impact of consumer culture, you can gain a clearer sense of what truly brings happiness and fulfillment. Remember, luxury is ultimately a personal choice. The goal isn't to reject it entirely but to approach it mindfully, making choices that reflect your authentic self rather than external pressures.

As you move forward, use these reflections to shape a life that feels rich—not in possessions, but in purpose, connection, and peace. True luxury is the freedom to live a life that aligns with who you are and what you genuinely value.

References and Sources

Books

- Baudrillard, Jean. *The Consumer Society: Myths and Structures.* SAGE Publications, 1998.
- Veblen, Thorstein. *The Theory of the Leisure Class.* Oxford University Press, 2007.
- Twitchell, James B. *Living It Up: Our Love Affair with Luxury.* Columbia University Press, 2002.
- Packard, Vance. *The Status Seekers.* David McKay Company, 1959.

Journal Articles

- Nunes, Joseph, and Xavier Dreze. "The Endowed Progress Effect: How Artificial Advancement Increases Effort." *Journal of Consumer Research*, vol. 32, no. 4, 2006, pp. 504-512.
- Chandon, Pierre, and Brian Wansink. "When Are Stockpiled Products Consumed Faster? A Convenience-Salience Framework of Post-Purchase Consumption Incidence and Quantity." *Journal of Marketing Research*, vol. 39, no. 3, 2002, pp. 321-335.

Industry Reports

- Bain & Company. *Global Luxury Goods Market Report 2022.* Bain & Company, 2022.
- McKinsey & Company. *The State of Fashion 2023: An In-Depth Look at Trends in the Luxury Goods Sector.* McKinsey & Company, 2023.

Websites and Online Sources

- "The Psychology Behind Why People Buy Luxury Goods." *Psychology Today*. Available at: www.psychologytoday.com/us/articles/why-we-buy-luxury.
- Wolf, Cam. "How Social Media Turned Luxury into a Basic Necessity." *GQ*, 14 Oct. 2020. Available at: www.gq.com/story/social-media-luxury-goods.
- "Luxury Goods Market Size, Share & Trends Analysis Report by Product." *Grand View Research*, 2023. Available at: www.grandviewresearch.com.

Statistics and Data Sources

- Statista. *India's Growing Middle Class and Luxury Spending Habits*. Statista, 2023.
- Euromonitor International. *Global Consumer Trends 2023*. Euromonitor International, 2023.

Documentaries

- *The True Cost*. Directed by Andrew Morgan, Life Is My Movie Entertainment, 2015.
- *The Price of Everything*. Directed by Nathaniel Kahn, HBO, 2018.

Interviews and Personal Communications

- Patel, Radhika. Personal interview. 5 March 2024.
- Sharma, Arun. "Luxury and the Indian Middle Class." Phone interview. 12 July 2024.

Market Studies and Influencer Impact

- "How Influencers Shape Luxury Brand Preferences Among Young Consumers." *Influencer Marketing Hub*, 2023.
- Raconteur. "Luxury Market Evolution and the New Consumer Class." *Raconteur*, 2022.